Amphibious Warfare in World War II: The History and Legacy of the War's Most Important Landing Operations

By Charles River Editors

Canadian troops in Sicily after the amphibious invasion

About Charles River Editors

Charles River Editors is a boutique digital publishing company, specializing in bringing history back to life with educational and engaging books on a wide range of topics. Keep up to date with our new and free offerings with this 5 second sign up on our weekly mailing list, and visit Our Kindle Author Page to see other recently published Kindle titles.

We make these books for you and always want to know our readers' opinions, so we encourage you to leave reviews and look forward to publishing new and exciting titles each week.

Introduction

A picture of Allied troops unloading supplies during the invasion of Sicily

Amphibious Warfare in World War II

A swift, sudden attack from the ocean, putting soldiers ashore on a hostile coast at some point weakly defended by the enemy, has been a powerful tactical and strategic tool since the late Bronze Age. Utilized by the Sea Peoples against New Kingdom Egypt and the Greek city-states in their internecine wars, amphibious warfare combined high mobility with a strong chance of complete surprise.

The technique continued in use through such periods as the early Medieval era, when Viking armies numbering up to 10,000 men struck suddenly and devastatingly from the sea using their highly seaworthy longships or "dragonships" (drekkar). At around the same time, the Normans carried out amphibious landings of invasion forces, including mounted men, in Muslim-occupied Sicily (1061) and Saxon England (1066).

As navies grew larger and the Spanish clashed with the Turks in the Mediterranean during the Renaissance, some military forces introduced specialized marines for the first time. These men, trained specially for landings carried out using ships' boats, formed a part of many European navies from the 16th century onward.

World War II, however, witnessed a sudden explosion in the scope and metamorphosis in the methods of amphibious warfare. With battlefields covering significant portions of the planetary surface, combined with the availability of the modern era's powerful technology and vehicles, the mighty conflict witnessed tactical and strategic amphibious operations unlike any the world had seen before.

All major powers involved in the war utilized amphibious operations to one degree or another. Even the Soviets launched more than 150 amphibious assaults during the war, albeit with very mixed success given the lack of dedicated landing craft and their variable troop quality. However, as the war continued, the United States developed the largest and most sophisticated assortment of amphibious warfare tactics, strategies, and equipment. The invasion of Sicily in 1943 was the largest amphibious operation in history, but it would be dwarfed on June 6, 1944. That day, forever known as D-Day, the Allies commenced Operation Overlord by staging the largest and most complex amphibious invasion in human history. The complex operation would require tightly coordinated naval and air bombardment, paratroopers, and even inflatable tanks that would be able to fire on fortifications from the coastline, all while landing over 150,000 men across nearly 70 miles of French beaches. Given the incredibly complex plan, it's no surprise that Supreme Commander Dwight D. Eisenhower had already written a letter apologizing for the failure of the invasion, which he carried in his coat pocket throughout the day.

Ultimately, amphibious operations at places like Okinawa, Iwo Jima, and various parts of Europe determined the course of the war, and *Amphibious Warfare in World War II: The History and Legacy of the War's Most Important Landing Operations* examines these crucial events. Along with pictures of important people, places, and events, you will learn about World War II's amphibious warfare like never before.

Early German Assaults

While the Germans pioneered some techniques of amphibious warfare during their early offensives at the start of the war, they never developed large-scale amphibious branches in the manner of the Soviets, Japanese, and Americans. The Wehrmacht remained an overwhelmingly land-based military whose main interaction with water consisted of engineers building pontoon bridges over rivers, a task at which the Germans frequently excelled.

Nevertheless, a few amphibious assaults occurred at the start of Operation Barbarossa, with the Germans attacking several large islands off the coast of the Baltic states to deny their use to the Soviets. Just as the Fall Rot attack through the Ardennes into France in 1940 repeated the Imperial German offensive through the same forest during World War I (and a third attempt via the same route would result in the Battle of the Bulge in 1944), so the seizure of the Baltic Islands in 1941 mirrored a nearly identical, if more primitively equipped, Imperial German amphibious assault in World War I.

The landings targeted the islands of Ösel, Dagö and Moon, which also bear the names of Saarema, Hiluma, and Muhu respectively. The Germans developed two plans for the assault, Operations Beowulf I and Beowulf II. In the event, the rapid seizure of Estonia allowed them to use the Beowulf II operational plan, an attack from the east launched from Estonia's western coast across the Great Sound.

The islands presented some difficult terrain features despite mostly being a few feet above sea level, sparsely inhabited with some small towns and farmland. In some areas, stable sand dunes 150 to 225 feet high occurred, creating an approximation of hilly terrain. Thick coniferous forest covered much of the land area. However, they had relatively high military value – the Soviets had built a large aerodrome at Möonuste, and a combined port facility and airbase at Papisaare, both on the island of Ösel.

The Germans noted other possible impediments besides the 15 Soviet coastal batteries defending the islands: "The islands of Ösel and Dagö are strongly fortified. The shores and islands of the entire Baltic Sea region have been developed for naval defense. For this purpose, the islands as well as the bays of the coast and the coast itself offer favorable preconditions. The narrow access roads can be easily secured by mine barriers." (Melzer, 1960, 24).

In order to increase their chances of success, the Germans planned no less than three diversionary landings in addition to the actual assault, "Northwind," "Southwind," and "Westwind." Finnish ships would provide the forces for Northwind, allowing the Germans to concentrate more of their own craft for the other feints and main attack.

The Soviet garrison consisted of approximately 20,000 men in all, 1,000 on Moon, 7,000 on Dagö, and 12,000 on the island of Ösel. The Germans committed two infantry divisions of the

Wehrmacht – the 61st and the 217th, the latter held in reserve. A battalion of "Green Devil" Fallschirmjagers joined these units. Elements of the 1st Luftflotte (Air Fleet) of the Luftwaffe would support the attack, and a large number of vessels made up the armada assigned to Operation Beowulf II. Georg von Kuchler commanded.

Along with dozens of larger craft, the 61st Infantry Division would use 123 squad-sized assault boats and 26 Siebel ferries – bizarre but practical motorized landing craft mounting a large central platform atop two catamaran-style pontoons, which could transport artillery, vehicles, and troops as needed. Many were also armed with 88mm FlaK cannons for protection against air attack as well as direct fire at shore emplacements.

The troops gathered to their staging points near Werder under cover of darkness on September 13, 1941. Despite the murkiness of the night, the Wehrmacht soldiers prepared for the attack with quiet efficiency, thankful for the lack of Soviet bombardment: "Paths and drainage ditches were hardly recognizable in the very dark night. While enemy artillery fire had frequently hit Werder and the surrounding area on the days before, the night of 13 to 14 September was quiet. Only enemy headlights shone from the island of Moon across to the mainland. The assault boats were loaded with people and material until 4 o'clock; PaK [field guns] were loaded on big pontoon rafts and attached to the stormboats. The loading of the first wave proceeded according to plan, so that, even in total darkness, it launched from the shore at 4 o'clock." (Melzer, 1960, 40).

The night suddenly erupted into a pealing cacophony of thunder as German batteries launched a preparatory bombardment towards the island shore. For 35 minutes, explosions rocked the darkened coast, filling the night with fire, smoke, plumes of earth and stone, and lethally whining shell fragments. As the last echoes died away, the snarl of dozens of assault boat motors sprang to life, and the Germans moved inshore to the attack. The first wave miscalculated its direction and came ashore two miles south of its intended landing zone, near the Soviet base at Kuivastu. The Germans immediately came under heavy machine gun fire as they splashed ashore, followed by shelling from the Soviet batteries. The second wave of Wehrmacht men landed at the correct point, encountering less resistance there, but found their landing delayed by an hour due to rough seas.

The battalions near Kuivastu began taking heavy casualties from the Soviet fire, but they fought their way inland doggedly, pushing the Soviets back several hundred yards from the beach. The land-based German batteries attempted supporting fire but their rounds fell short, striking their own assault troops. A hasty radio call silenced the battery fire.

As the morning dawned, Luftwaffe aircraft came to the attackers' aid, with Bf 109 and Bf 110 fighters strafing Soviet positions and Stuka dive-bombers making their bombing runs with Jericho trumpets howling. Several Kriegsmarine naval destroyers, now able to clearly see the Soviet positions in the morning light, opened fire with their guns, providing a direct artillery barrage which devastated Soviet machine gun and artillery positions, smashing weapons and blowing crews into bloody fragments.

Engineers crawled forward to clear lanes through Soviet minefields. Working together smoothly, the 61st Infantry troops, Luftwaffe, and destroyers systematically drove the Soviet troops back into the large island's interior, though the Russians continued to fight back with great courage. By nightfall on the 14th, the Germans had established a bridgehead approximately 3.5 miles long but with considerably less depth. A violent swell rising on the ocean prevented the third and later waves from landing.

On September 15th, the Germans and Finns undertook the three diversionary feints of Northwind, Southwind, and Westwind. These efforts had the desired result, with the Soviets rushing troops to all of the apparently threatened points. The diversionary forces then retreated without loss, with the exception of a Finnish vessel which struck a Soviet sea mine and sank north of the islands.

Over the next few days, Siebel ferries landed the rest of the 61st Infantry Division, as well as self-propelled assault guns, halftracks, and towed artillery. Moving systematically through the islands, the Germans reduced one Soviet strongpoint after another, using close cooperation between infantry, assault guns, aircraft, and, where possible, destroyers and cruisers providing artillery support from offshore.

By October 21st, the Germans rooted out the last pockets of resistance on all three islands, gaining control of the airfields and port facilities. At a cost of 2,850 WIA, MIA, and KIA, the Wehrmacht killed approximately 5,000 of the defending Soviets and captured 15,000 – a notable achievement considering that the Soviets enjoyed a 2:1 numerical superiority against the German amphibious forces that actually landed on the islands.

Soviet Amphibious Doctrine

Soviet amphibious warfare theory and doctrine stretched back to the later 1930s, well before the start of World War II. Though quite detailed and in some ways as sophisticated as the doctrine of any other major military power, a serious disconnect existed between theory and practice. While leading Soviet naval thinkers developed detailed strategies and tactics for using landing craft, no Russian-made landing craft actually existed. In essence, the amphibious warfare branch existed as a head without a body.

Even when the deadly demands of actual invasion of Soviet territory forced the Soviet fleet to bring their ideas into reality, at least in some form, to counter the hard-driving offensives of the Wehrmacht, the situation had changed little. Soviet leaders found themselves trying to shoehorn more or less sound tactical plans into the extreme practical constraints of the equipment available to them – small boats, motorized rafts, even oar-propelled barges. For this reason, among others, some Soviet amphibious operations yielded surprising levels of success, but many others came to grief in spectacular fashion. Nevertheless, the Soviet marines and naval infantry would win the grudgingly respectful nickname of "Striped Death" from the Germans – referring both to their striped naval shirts and to their aggressive fighting spirit.

From the start, the Soviets developed a slightly divergent idea of amphibious operations than that created by the U.S. Navy. The American concept focused entirely on seaborne coastal landings, whether on islands or on the continental shore. The Soviet military men, by contrast, deemed any attack over water qualified as an amphibious operation. Thus, they tried to devise tactics that would work equally well on rivers and lakes as along the seacoast.

This doctrinal focus even appeared in the USSR's official definition of amphibious operations: "An amphibious operation is an action coordinated and connected by a unified concept and plan for landing the amphibious forces on a hostile shore and for fulfilling their combat mission there." (Military Publishing House, 1983, 458). This definition both helped and hindered Soviet amphibious actions during World War II. On the ledger's positive side, it meant that planners put as much energy and detail into freshwater assaults as they did into ocean shore landings. Conversely, the very different conditions along rivers and lakes, and the open ocean, made it more difficult to come up with a set of concepts and tactics that would work well in both situations.

The roots of Soviet amphibious tactics grew in the blood-soaked soil of the Russian Civil War. The communist Reds launched several amphibious assaults against the Whites, creating a small but significant body of practical knowledge to draw from. Admiral Ivan Isakov, a veteran of some very early amphibious assaults during both World War I and the Russian Civil War, wrote a treatise on the subject in 1931. This document served as the blueprint for Soviet amphibious doctrine in World War II also – unsurprising since Isakov received the rank of Chief of Staff of Soviet naval forces for the conflict's duration.

ПОЧТА СССР 1974

4 К

АДМИРАЛ ФЛОТА СОВЕТСКОГО СОЮЗА
И.С.ИСАКОВ
1894-1967

Isakov

Soviet amphibious operations fell into three categories by Isakov's definition, all of which could be executed over any large body of water – rivers, larger lakes, or the ocean. The smallest, raids, consisted of small-scale spoiling attacks to confuse the enemy, cause them to waste time and resources, or achieve limited objectives such as destroying a hostile supply depot. Tactical operations supported larger land-based offensives or defensive operations, using battalion to division-sized forces. Strategic operations consisted of the main thrust of an attack, using a force anywhere from corps to army size.

The Soviets named various units "marines" and "naval infantry," though little difference existed between the two. They saw employment in entirely land-based battles also when the need for manpower overrode the inclination to preserve their rather sketchy specialized training for amphibious operations. Amphibious operations also made use of regular "land" forces, with no particular training for coastal assaults.

Another Soviet idiosyncrasy emerged with the fact that Red Army generals from the land forces nominally always commanded amphibious operations, even when these involved nothing but naval infantry. In theory, high-ranking Soviet naval officers never commanded the actual landings – the navy's role consisted entirely of providing a "taxi service" to the scene of the attack, with no say over its location or the tactics used for the actual landing. However, in practice, admirals ended up exerting full command and control over amphibious attacks "by default," when no general officer reached the location on time or when they suffered incapacitating wounds in the field.

While the Soviets began amphibious operations as soon as late 1941, shortly after the German invasion in June, they did not begin landing rehearsals before an operation until 1943. The Germans, forward-thinking in this as in many (though not all) military matters, used landing rehearsals ahead of time to prepare their troops for the actual operation. The Americans soon learned the utility of rehearsals, too, while the Soviets and British lagged in this regard. But eventually, the Soviets recognized the advantage these practice runs gave and began making use of them as well. Despite this, their amphibious operations often had a very short planning and preparation time, ranging from a few hours to a few days before the shore attack actually began. Practically none of them received planning more than three weeks in advance, contributing to an *ad hoc* approach even with the best conceived and most thoroughly prepared landings.

The Soviets deployed a crazy collection of vessels for their landings, including navy ships, civilian fishing craft, scientific research boats from the prewar period, and any tugs, barges, or other floating objects readily to hand. Barges saw frequent use since they could transport large numbers of men, a few vehicles, and heavy weapons such as machine guns and large artillery pieces. These barges received the nickname "Bolinders" – the Swedish Bolinder company manufactured some of the barges, and the name soon applied to all such craft in Soviet service regardless of their origin.

The Russians used totally unarmored craft for the most part, and the actual shore approach took place either in Bolinders or small rowboats and ship's boats. These craft rarely mounted engines. The Soviets used oar power to bring the craft inshore, and photographs survive of large, long oars projecting from the sides of Bolinder barges, manned by naval infantry or regular Red Army soldiers. They also employed captured German amphibious assault barges, though never in large numbers.

These conditions, of course, made the troops extremely vulnerable to shore fire if they made a contested landing. Artillery, machine guns, and even rifle fire could play havoc with the unprotected "Striped Death" as they strained and sweated over their oars, more or less completely exposed. Nevertheless, successful landings still occurred, usually where the Soviets achieved surprise. On other occasions, the Soviet naval infantry and marines sustained ghastly casualty levels when caught by German artillery, machine gun fire, and strafing in their slow, fragile craft.

Late in the war, the Soviets received a large consignment of purpose-built armored landing craft from the Americans through the Lend-Lease program, via the Alaska route. The Soviets saw the value of these craft, as they did with U.S.-made airplanes, but by then the war against the Germans had moved away from the Black Sea coasts and transporting them overland from the Pacific made little sense. The Lend-Lease vessels included 2 LCVPs (Landing Craft Vehicle Personnel), 2 LCS (Landing Ship – Support), 56 LCMs (Landing Craft, Mechanized), 32 LCTs (Landing Craft, Tank), and 30 LCIs (Landing Craft, Infantry) in total. The Soviets slated these for use in the projected invasion of Japan in 1946, and actually employed a few during their 1945 invasion of Manchuria and Korea, with several destroyed by Japanese artillery fire. For the most part, however, they never saw action beyond training exercises.

Like other nations, the Soviets used their naval vessels to give supporting fire to landings. They also operated "river monitors" – gunboats, typically converted from fishing and survey craft – on major rivers, especially the Dniepr, along with lakes. On the northern lakes, where the Finns and a number of German divisions attempted an attack through taiga and tundra through Murmansk, the Soviets sometimes used barges for surprise attacks, and on one occasion retreated across a lake using hundreds of makeshift rafts.

Major Soviet Amphibious Assaults

Out of the approximately 150 known Soviet amphibious assaults, most consisted of small-scale raids, and only a handful reached the scale of full operations, most of which were carried out by the Black Sea Fleet. The strategically important Crimea witnessed several of these landings.

The first Allied amphibious attack of World War II occurred on September 23rd, 1941 near Odessa, when the Soviets attempted to relieve the besieged city. The assault in this case developed amid tremendous confusion. The original leader of the attack could not direct it because a German U-boat fired torpedoes into his ship, wounding him badly enough to prevent his participation. With various other Army and Navy officers squabbling over the chain of command, Vice Admiral Sergey Gorshkov stepped in to actually command the landing.

Gorshkov

The Black Sea fleet picked up the 3rd Marine Regiment and other troops in Sevastapol and arrived off Grigorevka, east of Odessa, early in the morning of September 23rd. The Axis troops holding this sector consisted of two Romanian divisions. The Soviets intended to come ashore under cover of darkness and destroy the Romanian's artillery batteries, aimed towards Odessa.

In the chill autumn darkness, the first of two waves of men totaling 1,920 Soviet marines climbed down swaying rope ladders from the decks of their transporting cruisers to waiting barges and motor craft. In all, 19 motor boats and 10 barges made up the attack force. As each boat filled, it moved away from the looming bulk of the warship across the inky water towards the dark, silent Crimean shore.

As the boats carried the first wave towards the beach, immense flashes of light suddenly split the night apart as the heavy guns of the cruisers opened fire. Shells screamed overhead to land thunderously on the shoreline, pounding the dark coast where Romanian soldiers might be waiting with machine guns and artillery for the Soviets to close in. The shock of the guns firing rolled across the water's surface as the Russian marines strained their eyes into the darkness ahead, searching for the first responding muzzle flash. They saw nothing except the bursts of exploding shells, however.

The cruisers' guns hammered the landing area for nine minutes, then fell silent. The first Soviet troops jumped into the surf and waded ashore at around 0200 hours, only to discover that – anticlimactically but probably to their great relief – that no enemy troops awaited them. The attack had achieved complete tactical surprise.

Contributing to its success, several aircraft dropped 25 Soviet paratroopers a few miles inland from the landing zone. These men landed almost directly on a Romanian command post. Gunning down its occupants, the paratroopers attacked other Romanian units nearby, creating utter chaos that prevented the Romanian troops from counterattacking the landing, or perhaps even realizing that it took place.

They learned of the new threat soon enough, however, as the Soviet marines organized themselves and launched an attack on their primary objective, the Romanian artillery positions. With the Romanians still off-balance, the Soviet troops succeeded in destroying the batteries, then linking up with Odessa's defenders.

In mid-October, the Soviet High Command decided to abandon Odessa and use the troops there to reinforce the more significant defensive position of Sevastopol. Once again, Gorshkov put his small armada into action, this time using the barges and motor boats to successfully evacuate most of the remaining Odessa garrison and the 3rd Marine Regiment.

During Operation Silver Fox, the German invasion of extreme northern European Russia from Finland, battalion-sized or company-sized units of Soviet marines and naval infantry landed on the shores of the Arctic Ocean. Operating in brutally demanding conditions even in the region's summer – just like the elite German Gebirgsjager or mountain troops opposing them – these men nevertheless proved their fighting spirit and determination repeatedly. These small forays – "raiding" operations by Isakov's classification, with small numbers and short duration – did not actually halt the Germans, but they increased the "friction" of the German advance considerably. Though they generally defeated the Soviet naval infantry in direct encounters, the Germans found themselves compelled to detach units to guard their seaward flank, which decreased the men available for the forward drive towards Murmansk. Accordingly, the amphibious activities of these units represented one of a number of factors that caused the German advance to grind to a halt before it could reach its objective and sever one of the important Lend-Lease routes into the Soviet Union.

The Crimea continued to be the main focus for Soviet amphibious actions throughout the war, thanks to its long Black Sea coastline. The relative ease of naval operations in the region compared to those in the subarctic also contributed to its prominence for these landings. After the limited but successful September landing at Odessa, the Soviets tried again in December near Sevastopol, with very different results.

The Soviets planned the Kerch-Feodosiya Landing Operation to strike at the 11th Army of Erich von Manstein, encircling Sevastopol, in late December 1941. The Germans intercepted a spike of radio messages, which, combined with other intelligence, gave them forewarning of the operation and greatly reduced the Soviet advantage of surprise. The Soviets mustered over

42,000 men for the assault, bringing reinforcements on the cruisers "Krasnyi Krym" and "Krasnyi Kavkaz" ("Red Crimea" and "Red Caucasus"). As usual, the operation began in darkness to give the men going ashore better protection from German and Romanian fire. The attack launched at 0350 on December 28th, 1941, aiming to take the Kerch Peninsula and from there break the German siege of Sevastopol. Conditions proved brutal but provided visual cover for the amphibious forces: "But the other impediments to an amphibious assault, namely choppy seas, tumbling surf, and cold, rainy weather, were waiting along the entire Crimean coast. The operation was the largest and most complex amphibious assault conducted by the Soviets in the entire war." (Atwater, 1995, Web).

Attacking steep, mountainous terrain at Feodosiya, the main Soviet landing met stiff resistance from the German troops there, despite their relatively low numbers. Luftwaffe pilots braved the gale-force winds and blackness to strafe the Soviet troops as they struggled ashore, while Wehrmacht small arms and artillery fire hammered the landing zone. Nevertheless, the Soviets stubbornly continued their landing. As the hours passed and more and more Russians forced their way ashore at Feodosiya, the German commander at Kerch, Hans Graf von Sponeck, disobeyed direct orders and moved most of his men to support the Feodosiya defenders.

However, at this time, a second Soviet amphibious landing began at Kerch, with 5,000 men of the 83rd Marine Brigade followed up by elements of the Soviet 51st Army. These troops successfully established a beachhead at Kerch despite incessant air attacks by the Luftwaffe. Sponeck's move of troops to Feodosiya relieved pressure on the Kerch landing, and both sites ended the day in Soviet hands, though it required 7 hours to put all the men ashore at Feodosiya in their storm-tossed rowboats.

Sponeck paid a surprisingly high price for his attempt to reinforce Feodosiya - his superiors sentenced him to death at a court-martial for disobeying orders. Hitler himself intervened, commuting the sentence to 7 years imprisonment, but in 1944, after the abortive assassination attempt on the Fuhrer, Himmler ordered Sponeck executed, for reasons which remain unclear considering that he had no connection to the plot.

For their part, the Soviets managed to seize the Kerch Peninsula and relieve pressure on Sevastopol for a time, as planned. However, with the return of warmer weather, Erich von Manstein launched a stunning counteroffensive in April 1942 that completely annihilated the units on the peninsula as well as many other Soviet forces in the Crimea.

Gorshkov, the same commander who oversaw these operations, also led the final major amphibious landing in Crimea by the Soviets, the Kerch-Eltigen Operation in 1943. At least 27,700 Soviet amphibious troops participated. The Axis forces consisted of Wehrmacht troops of the 5th Army, Gebirgsjagers, and the ferociously hard-fighting Romanian Vânători de Munte, or Mountain Huntsmen Corps, who proved their elite capabilities time and again during the various Crimean battles of World War II.

The assault began on October 31, 1943, with the troops sent off with a menacing lecture on the consequences of failure by Chief Political Commissar Leonid Brezhnev. The men crowded into nearly 300 motorized cutters and other motor craft, along with a chaotic array of sailboats, rowboats, barges, and even crudely constructed timber rafts. Insufficient boats led to overcrowding and the necessity of leaving all heavy weapons aboard ship.

The first echelon landing at Eltigen established a beachhead, but subsequent echelons experienced extreme difficulties, with craft overturned into the frigid water by massive waves while Stuka dive-bombers and other Luftwaffe aircraft made strafing runs. Even one of the assault leaders, Colonel Vasily Gladkov, found himself forced to wad ashore through bitterly cold, waist-deep water when his boat grounded hopelessly on a shoal. When he finally reached land, he found a diminutive naval infantry soldier regaling his comrades with what may very well have been a tall tale of his exploits:

"The soldiers from the 1st Battalion squatted down on their haunches, covering themselves with raincoats against the rain. Inside their close circle, the miniature figure of comrade Senior Sergeant Hadov, a member of the Novorossiysk landing party, a merry fellow, the favorite of the whole battalion, is barely visible. Hadov also tells a funny story: 'I burst into the house and dashed up the stairs. Suddenly I meet a gigantic fascist. A whole mountain, what they would call a 'berg.' I have zero height next to him, coming up to his waist. He will crush me with a fingernail. What to do? I rush at him in desperation and knock him head over heels. Fritz falls over the banister and hangs there head-down, his pants snagged on the railing. Of course, I have to 'help' the poor fellow. His pants remained intact, but I can't say the same for him...'" And again the laughter of listeners covers the words of the narrator. And it seems that the wind is softer and the sea is not so gloomy." (Gladkov, 1972, 45).

Regardless of whether Hadov actually sent an opponent hurtling to his death by unfastening his pants so that he slipped out of them and fell down a stairwell, many more "fascists" of all sizes soon closed in on the landing area. The Soviet troops at Eltigen fought hard, but could not push further than roughly a mile inland due to stubborn resistance. The amphibious troops soon found themselves surrounded and under siege. German naval ships blockaded the seaward approach, while Luftwaffe aircraft shot down many of the planes sent in a desperate effort to resupply to surrounded men.

The siege ended on December 6-7, when the Romanians launched a two-pronged attack on the isolated beachhead. The 6th Cavalry Division provided a diversion, whereupon the tough Mountain Huntsmen Corps attacked from the west, supported by StuG III assault guns, and systematically rolled up the Soviet position. 1,200 Soviets died and another 1,570 surrendered. 820 marines and naval infantry fought their way clear of the trap and took refuge on Mount Mithridates, destroying Wehrmacht artillery batteries located there. The men of the Romanian 3rd Mountain Division undertook to root these Soviet escapees out, but at least some managed to evacuate by sea on ships sent to their rescue by Admiral Glashkov. The Romanians captured or killed the rest by December 11.

While the Eltigen landing ended in disaster, the Yenikale landing close to Kerch enjoyed much greater success, ranking as the Soviets' most effective amphibious operation of the war. The 98th Infantry Division of the Wehrmacht under General Martin Gereis bore the brunt of this assault, which the Soviets carried out under cover of heavy smokescreens. The Soviet landing forces managed to establish a beachhead in part because many of the 98th Infantry Divisions *landsers* had been sent to aid the Romanians at Eltigen.

Eventually, the Soviets managed to push no less than 75,000 men ashore at Yenikale, along with 128 tanks, 582 artillery pieces, and over 700 trucks. In spring 1944, the Soviets broke out from this massive beachhead and began the campaign which would expel the Wehrmacht permanently from the Crimea. Due to its success, the Yenikale landing became a primary example for Soviet staff college study in the postwar years.

Amphibious operations once again came to the fore in the far north in late 1944, when the Soviets launched the Kirkenes-Petsamo operation against German and Finnish forces. The two sides had faced one another in an uneasy stalemate since Operation Silver Fox fizzled out in autumn of 1941. Now, the Red Army began an offensive under cover of bad Arctic Circle weather, including amphibious operations along the Barents Sea coast.

The assault commenced on October 7th, 1944, with 98,806 Soviet soldiers advancing against 56,000 Germans in terms of the whole front, giving the Soviets odds of 1.7:1 overall. However, main Soviet drive – what the Germans would term the *Schwerpunkt* – concentrated 69,652 Red Army troops against just 16,026 Gebirgsjager and other German soldiers, providing a ratio of 4.3:1. The Soviets also made full use of the local conditions: "On the day of the offensive, the weather conditions generally favored the attacking Soviet infantry. Wind from the north was bringing fog to all the low areas and occasional mist to the high ground. Visibility, however, was a problem, due to the low cloud cover and falling snow. The artillery preparation began as scheduled at 0800, and in two and one half hours, the Soviets fired more than 100,000 rounds." (Gebhardt, 1989, 31).

The Soviet 14th Army under Lieutenant General V.L. Shcherbakov found themselves pitted against the Wehrmacht's XIX Mountain Corps, consisting of several Gebirgsjager divisions. The Soviets advanced across the painfully broken terrain with its sharp ridges, ravines, and numerous small, marshy rivers, alternating between tundra and thick, gnarled stands of trees.

Almost immediately, the Soviets began amphibious landings of Naval Infantry brigades along the Barents Sea coast. These men fought their way inland against heavy German resistance, though their local odds of 2.7:1 allowed them to maintain forward pressure despite the Gebirgsjager's determination. In at least one instance, the tough Soviet marines advanced grimly over a major German minefield covered in 10 inches of fresh snow, which made minesweeping all but impossible with the equipment available.

The Soviets made five landings in all between the Rybachii Peninsula (which means the "Fisherman's Peninsula" and which the Germans referred to as Fischerhals) and Varanger Peninsula and Fjord to the west. This effectively outflanked the German defensive positions and put some 11,000 Soviet naval infantry and marines ashore against 4,000 Wehrmacht men assigned to coastal guard duty.

With no purpose-built landing craft available, the disembarkation proved extremely slow. Getting soaked in the freezing cold Barents Sea water could easily lead to incapacitated or even dead Soviet soldiers from hypothermia, even with heavy Soviet winter gear, due to the searingly cold northern winds blowing from the Arctic. For this reason, the Soviets did not simply wade ashore but pulled their boats in as close as possible, then ran out long wooden gangplanks to the beach.

This forced the Soviet troops to file ashore slowly. Since a counterattack at this point could be fatal, the Soviets conducted the landings during the hours of darkness, choosing points where they correctly guessed no German troops awaited them. German coastal batteries endured heavy counterbattery fire from Soviet land batteries, preventing them from shelling the landing barges effectively. In some cases, the naval infantry used makeshift log rafts to reach the shore.

These amphibious assaults fell into Isakov's second category of landings, those of tactical landings to support a main land-based offensive. Given their poor equipment, the Soviet amphibious troops performed superbly, landing successfully on a hostile shore and heavily harassing the Germans' seaward flank. The Wehrmacht responded aggressively, as the 20th Mountain Army's war diary described via transcription of a conversation between two German commanders: "Chief of Staff, XIX Mountain Corps: 'The enemy is conducting landings on both sides of Fischerhals [Rybachii Peninsula].' Chief of Staff, 20th Mountain Army: 'The landing at the sea narrows of not of long-range significance; therefore, concentrate all your assets against the landing west of Fischerhals, in order to throw the enemy back.'" (Gebhardt, 1989, 91-92).

The 20th Mountain Army's chief of staff actually assessed the landings correctly when he declared them not of long-range significance, though perhaps for reasons he did not anticipate. While the Soviet naval infantry fought bravely, with one man, Senior Sergeant I.P. Katorzhnyi, winning the Hero of the Soviet Union award for his valor, the clumsy, uncoordinated command structure of the Red Army totally prevented coordination between the naval infantry and the ground forces.

Further hampering the Soviet operations, all reinforcement requests for the landings needed approval from STAVKA supreme headquarters in Moscow. Far removed from the scene of the fighting, the top brass could not make the same informed judgments as the officers on the ground. Requests to land reinforcements at Petsamo at a crucial moment led to STAVKA sending the reinforcing naval infantry to another landing site entirely, one where they remained useless for much of the offensive.

The operation ended in victory for the Soviets, but the initial plan of surrounding the Germans by using the naval infantry to envelop their positions failed entirely. The Gebirgsjager, finally defeated after more than a week of extremely heavy fighting during which the Soviets almost failed when shoddy logistics starved their front-line men of small arms ammunition for several days, successfully withdrew to the west. The amphibious operation showed every sign of good planning, and the men carrying it succeeded in its opening phases, but interference by remote high command and deeply flawed local command structures preventing coordination between various elements of the offensive squandered its potential almost entirely.

Several small but seriously attempted Soviet amphibious attacks in the Baltic states came to grief in the war's latter years. Faced by tough German and Baltic veterans fighting desperately on the defensive, the Soviet troops suffered annihilation more than once under the cold skies and beside the deep blue waters of the Baltic region.

In 1944, a battalion of 525 Soviet naval infantry landed at Mereküle in Estonia, only to find themselves attacked by two companies of Estonian Waffen SS. The hard-fighting Estonians killed or captured 500 of the Soviets while sustaining far fewer casualties, illustrating the risks of amphibious operations against a shore defended by determined and militarily skilled adversaries.

Japanese Operations

The Japanese were the pioneers of a new type of landing craft – purpose-built, armored, frequently armed amphibious assault vessels with a ramp at the prow that served both as a massive shield for the craft's occupants during the approach to the beach and as a stable gangplank or unloading ramp once dropped on arrival. The Americans subsequently observed the idea, copied it, and developed it into even more effective forms.

Japanese landing craft first saw large-scale service during the Second Sino-Japanese War in 1937. Making beach landings on the coast of China, the Japanese needed a method of moving their ferocious infantry ashore alive in the teeth of heavy Chinese small arms fire. As Soviet experiences showed, amphibious landings carried out with slow, unarmored craft only had a chance of success if they landed at weakly defended points. The new armored, motorized Japanese landing craft with integrated ramps opened up vast stretches of coast to attack which no unarmored craft could hope to approach without being destroyed, or at least losing most of the men on board. This large boost to tactical and strategic flexibility represented the next evolution of amphibious warfare.

The creation of armored landing craft even made daytime amphibious assaults feasible. As the

German Baltic operations showed, even the Wehrmacht – more skilled and highly trained than the Soviets – only used their "storm-boats" and Siebel ferries at night in most instances, which exposed them to the risk of landing in the wrong location, being struck by their own supporting artillery, and other problems. Of course, moving into position at night remained crucial for surprise, but the ability to survive rifle and machine gun fire even in broad daylight created a host of fresh operational possibilities.

Conversely, the Japanese developed several types of landing craft for various tasks during daytime operations, and interestingly, the Imperial Japanese Navy did not control either the development or use of landing craft: "The Navy provided escort craft and conducted the invasion force to the pre-selected anchorage. From then on the Army took over completely. All the landing craft and ships used for landing troops and their equipment were designed and built under Army supervision, and were wholly manned by Army personnel." (Merriam, 2006, viii).

The Japanese developed five main types of landing craft, though very small numbers of other landing craft – some of them bizarre experimental types – also underwent construction. These included the *Chu Hatsu*, a small landing craft; the *Moku Hatsu*, a 50-foot, unarmored, all wood landing craft used exclusively for resupply and cargo hauling; the *Sho Hatsu*, a 35-foot steel landing craft with no ramp, designed for personnel; and the *Toku Dai Hatsu*, a 60-foot steel craft capable of carrying one medium tank or two light tanks. The Japanese built mostly *Dai Hatsu* type landing craft, however, which accounted for 85% of their landing craft fleet. 48 feet long, it could carry 10 tons of supplies, a number of troops, or a single light tank or truck. Powered by an 80 horsepower kerosene engine, it moved at a top speed of just over 9 mph. Its 86 mile range gave it considerable tactical mobility. The craft featured a folding ramp, welded steel sides, and a wooden deck for buoyancy, cheapness, and conservation of precious steel resources.

The Japanese also developed amphibious assault ships, leading the world in producing the first landing craft carriers. These ships featured the capacity to carry 54 landing craft plus 4 supporting armored gun boats, and included a well deck. This deck could be flooded immediately before action, allowing the landing craft to launch quickly out of the carrier under their own power rather than being individually launched, started, and loaded with a crane. Needless to say, all of this greatly increased the speed with which they entered action.

U.S. Navy Observers and Higgins Boats

Since hostilities between the United States and Japan lay well in the future in 1937, U.S. Navy observers in Shanghai had the opportunity to see and photograph the Japanese landing craft firsthand. These men recognized the potential military value of such intelligence, particularly since the USN spent much of the 1930s casting about for a landing craft design. Accordingly, they sent a number of reports on the Japanese landing craft back to the United States.

Victor H. Krulak of the U.S. Marines, along with USN fleet intelligence officer George A.

Phelan and a nameless USN photographer with an early telephoto lens on his camera, obtained Japanese permission to take a tugboat and watch a Japanese amphibious assault at Liuho on the Yangtze River. Phelan and Krulak, both extremely excited at the prospect of seeing this event, sailed their tugboat in close, completely ignored by the Japanese troops: "We watched troops debarking into boats from transports. We watched destroyers deliver naval gunfire on the beach [...] Most important, we got close enough to take close-up photographs of the Japanese assault landing craft. And there we saw, in action, exactly what the Marines had been looking for – sturdy, ramp-bow-type capable of transporting heavy vehicles and depositing them directly on the beaches. What we saw was that the Japanese were light-years ahead of us in landing craft design." (Krulak, 1984, 90).

Krulak

The men photographed the landing craft in action, prepared sketches illustrating the technical use of the craft and their tactics in landing on the beach, and wrote avid reports to send back to the United States. The two young officers believed themselves in possession of an intelligence coup which would revolutionize American amphibious warfare immediately.

However, when Krulak returned to America in summer of 1939 after spending two more years reporting on naval developments in the Sino-Japanese War, he discovered that not a single landing craft had been planned or built, even experimentally. Accordingly, he investigated, and he later recalled, "I spent a day hunting for my report in the files of the Navy's Bureau of Ships. Finally unearthed, I was chagrined to read a marginal comment from some bureau skeptic that the report was the work of 'some nut out in China.'" (Krulak, 1984, 91).

Nevertheless, Krulak continued to push his information on both the Navy and Marine Corps. The Navy itself largely ignored him, but he found a more receptive audience among the Marines. The final ingredient of the mix proved to be a loudmouthed, whiskey-drinking Louisianan of Irish descent, Andrew Higgins, a boat builder. Higgins had little regard for bureaucratic red tape or even the law, highlighted by the fact that he avoided bankruptcy and established the finances of his business by building shallow-draft wooden boats specifically for the use of rum runners in Louisiana's swamps and bayous during Prohibition. Higgins knew Marine Brigadier General E.P. Moses and Major Ernest E. Linsert, and these men, impressed by Krulak's and Phelan's reports, showed him the photographs and sketches of the Japanese landing craft.

Higgins

A period of development followed, resulting in the "Higgins boat," or LCVP – Landing Craft, Vehicle and Personnel. This 36-foot long all-steel ramp-bow craft featured a maximum draft of just three feet, making it highly maneuverable inshore. Armed with two .30-caliber machine guns and crewed by four men, it could carry 36 soldiers or a single vehicle weighing up to 6,000 lbs. This landing craft, a hybrid between Higgins' rum-running boat design and Japanese landing craft, became the workhorse of American amphibious landings during the war. In all, Higgins' company built 20,000 LCVPs.

A Higgins boat at Okinawa

American landing craft types proliferated from this point to the end of the war. U.S. engineers developed various specialized craft to address different tasks in the complex execution of a full-scale amphibious landing. Some types, including the LCVP, saw use throughout the entire war, while the Americans phased out others once they designed and manufactured better designs.

Higgins also produced the small LCP (Landing Craft Personnel) and the large LCM (Landing Craft Mechanized). Another variant included the LCP(L), or Landing Craft Personnel, Large, an upgraded steel version of the Higgins Eureka boat: "The original Eureka boat had a covered cabin and was built of wood, a commodity readily available in the southern United States. The boat had a shallow 18-inch draft and because of the 'headlog' – a solid block of pine at the bow –

enabled the boat to move at flank speed over obstacles with little or no damage. The bow design became known as a 'spoonbill' type because of its resemblance to the shallow wading bird." (Adcock, 2003, 7).

A picture of an LCPL at Guadalcanal

The LCP(R) or Landing Craft Personnel Ramp incorporated a ramp, while the LCV (Landing Craft Vehicle) could haul five tons of cargo, a one-ton truck, or 36 men. These craft would eventually be mostly replaced by the LCVP.

The LCM (Landing Craft Mechanized), first used in 1943, proved to be another durable design, created in prototype form by Higgins in a period of 60 hours, and later produced by multiple companies. As the war progressed, the US developed new marks of the LCM, each one larger and better equipped than the last. LCMs continued in service well after World War II, with the LCM-8 (mark 8) still in use in the early 21st century. The LCT (Landing Craft Tank) began as a British design but later saw American service also.

The large bow-ramp LCI(L), or Landing Craft Infantry Large, could carry up to 200 men, as well as being manufactured in several armed versions, and became known collectively as the "Water Bug Navy" due to their busy 'scurrying' over the ocean surface.

Much larger landing craft eventually rolled off the production lines to carry large groups of men or whole platoons of vehicles ashore. The 203-foot LSM (Landing Ship Medium) carried five medium tanks, three heavy tanks, or larger numbers of smaller vehicles and equipment. A support variant, the LSM(R), bore a large battery of rockets with a range of up to 3 miles to provide heavy indirect fire support at close ranges to landing operations.

The 328-foot LST – Landing Ship Tank, sarcastically dubbed the "Large Slow Target" by its crews – featured two decks, a tank deck able to hold 2,100 tons of vehicles, and a weather deck above this. The weather deck served both to protect the vehicles from the elements and as a cargo platform, with an elevator allowing fast loading and unloading of the gear and supplies carried there. The USA made numerous variants of the LST, including floating repair facilities, transports for smaller landing craft equipped with davits and cranes, and even a miniature "aircraft carrier" version deploying 6 spotter planes.

Most larger landing craft made use of diesel engines, while the smaller landing craft featured a mix of diesel and gasoline engines depending on their variant. Crews (and passengers, if well-informed) greatly preferred the diesel types for a simple reason. If a weapon heavy enough to penetrate the armor struck the craft, gasoline often ignited, creating a raging, lethal inferno on board which burned men to death and made sinking a near certainty. Diesel, however, shows much greater resistance to ignition in such a situation, giving the landing craft's occupants a much improved chance of survival.

Guadalcanal

The Guadalcanal Campaign, which ran from August 1942 to February 1943, was a bitter and protracted struggle that also happened to be a strange and transitional confrontation quite unlike any other in the long Pacific War. In conjunction with the American victory at the Battle of Midway, Guadalcanal represented the crucial moment when the balance of power in the Pacific tipped in favor of the Allies, but the idea that Guadalcanal would be such a significant battle would have come as a surprise to military strategists and planners on both sides.

Nonetheless, by the time the Guadalcanal campaign was underway, it was a confrontation that neither side actively sought, but that both sides came to believe they could not afford to lose. When Allied forces landed on the island, it was an effort to deny the Japanese the use of the island and other nearby islands, but the Japanese defenders fought bitterly in an effort to push them off the island, resulting in a rather unique battle that consisted mostly of a Japanese offensive against Americans that invaded amphibiously and dug in. While the Americans closed the campaign with a substantial material advantage, the American garrison on Guadalcanal was initially undermanned and terribly undersupplied.

Eventually, nearly 100,000 soldiers fought on the island, and the ferocity with which the Japanese fought was a fitting prelude to campaigns like Iwo Jima and Okinawa. The campaign would include six separate naval battles, three large-scale land clashes, and almost daily skirmishing and shelling. Not surprisingly, the campaign exacted a heavy toll, with more than 60 ships sunk, more than 1200 aircraft destroyed, and more than 38,000 dead. While the Japanese and Americans engaged at sea and in the skies, of the 36,000 Japanese defenders on the ground, over 30,000 of them would be dead by the end of the Guadalcanal campaign, while the Americans lost about 7,000 killed.

With only a very short time to prepare for the landings, the Marines began an intensive program of live rehearsal at Koro in the Fiji Islands. Unlike the Soviets, who only began rehearsals very late in the war, the Americans recognized the pressing need for such practice runs from the first. Though some of the coxswains piloting the landing craft feared that they would suffer too much damage pushing over the coral reefs to be used in the actual assault, Rear Admiral Richmond K. Turner, who commanded the landing craft force, had different ideas. He insisted on a relentless program of rehearsal which initially slashed landing time by half. Still not satisfied, Turner demanded even more of his men, with the result that they began to consistently achieve landing times one-third as long as achieved during their initial rehearsal.

Phase one of the new American offensive began in the predawn hours of August 7, 1942, when troops from the First Marine Division, under Major General Archer Vandegrift, landed on Tulagi and the north shore of Guadalcanal. The Marines were undertrained, consisting mostly of young post-Pearl Harbor recruits, and they were also poorly equipped. They had arrived in New Zealand in June as a small, forward-positioned contingent not expected see actual combat until sometime in 1943, and their transports had not even been "combat loaded," meaning they could not be unloaded rapidly in support of an amphibious landing. Upon learning of their new mission, the Marines rushed to reload the transports, dramatically cutting stocks of food, supplies, and even ammunition to save time.

Men of the 2nd Marines landed unopposed and rapidly took their immediate objectives. At 0800, the 2nd Battalion of the 5th Marines (part of the 1st Marine Division) landed on Beach Blue on Tulagi, encountering no immediate resistance beyond the passive obstacle of a shallow coral ridge that blocked the landing craft and forced the men to wade ashore anywhere from 100 to 300 feet through chest-deep water.

Picture of amphibious crafts headed towards Guadalcanal

The main landing of the 1st and 3rd Battalions, 5th Marines, commanded by Colonel LeRoy Hunt, on the main island of Guadalcanal began at 0909, after a brief but intense preparatory bombardment. The men who clambered down the sides of the ships using cargo nets and into the landing craft expected fierce Japanese resistance. Instead, they found the beach undefended and moved inland to establish a beachhead. The landing area came to resemble a traffic jam rather than a scene of combat, as the overall Marine command, Alexander Vandegrift, later recounted: "In mid-afternoon I moved my CP ashore. Our landing craft picked its way through myriad traffic infesting the blue inshore waters to add cargo to cargo already piling alarmingly on the white sand beach. There in the humid heat Marines stripped to dungaree trousers were trying to cope with the boxes and crates that had to be manhandled out of the small boats, then carried up the beach and sorted into diverse supply dumps." (Vandegrift, 1964, 123).

The Japanese deemed the landing a brief raid and therefore withdrew to the forested hills inland, there to await the Americans' departure. The first amphibious landing carried out by American forces thus went unopposed, though the battle of Guadalcanal would soon erupt into savage violence.

While this rush to battle left the Americans dangerously under-supplied, it also helped them to seize an advantage that had done so much for the Japanese in their six-month advance: surprise. The Japanese construction troops on Guadalcanal, unaware of the American landing until the moment that covering fire from naval guns began raining down upon them, initially offered little resistance. Most simply retreated into the jungle. On Tulagi and the nearby islands of Gavutu and Tanambogo, however, the main Japanese force pushed back tenaciously against the Marines. Outnumbered and taken by surprise, the Japanese defenders fought virtually to the last man, extracting the maximum possible price for control of the islands. Altogether, only three of the 350 Japanese soldiers on Tulagi survived, and only 20 of the roughly 500 on Gavutu and Tanambogo survived, a grim taste of the brutal combat that would come to characterize the Guadalcanal Campaign and the war in the Pacific as a whole.

Left temporarily stranded by the withdrawal of their fleet, which suffered a stunning naval reverse, the US Marines held out against banzai attacks, artillery bombardment, and strafing. Once reinforced, they succeeded at wiping out the Japanese defenders in a bitter struggle which left 1,752 American soldiers and over 15,000 Japanese dead, with only around 1,000 Japanese willing to surrender. Vandegrift characterized the fighting as "a storming operation... unremitting and relentless... decided by the extermination of one or another of the adversaries engaged. Soldierly behavior was manifestwherever the enemy was encountered... and there was an unflinching willingness to accept the... hazards of close and sanguinary combat." (Griffith, 1980, 40).

A picture of Marines coming to shore on Guadalcanal on August 7

With that, the Americans learned both the strengths and weaknesses of their new approach. The impossibility of boat-type landing craft approaching beaches protected by shallow coral ridges, and the potential disaster ensuing if men waded ashore in the face of heavy enemy fire rather than approaching a deserted beach, highlighted the urgent need for tracked or wheeled amphibious tractors and other amphibious vehicles that could cross such obstacles.

The Landing Vehicle Tracked (LVT), known by such nicknames as the "amtrack," "Alligator," or "Gator," already existed at the time of the Guadalcanal landing. However, it saw use only as a resupply vehicle rather than an assault craft during this first encounter of the Solomon Islands Campaign. The amtrack would come into its own during after the Tarawa landings of 1943, when it first saw use as an assault craft. The up-armored and improved LVT-2 followed, deployed in ever greater numbers, and a version of the amtrack armed with a 75mm howitzer as an infantry close support vehicle, dubbed the Amtank, duly entered American service during and after the Marianas campaign.

Another critical piece of equipment, the DUKW-353 amphibious truck, saw its combat debut during Operation Husky in 1943 when the Allies landed on Sicily in the Mediterranean. However, it also saw extensive use in the Pacific subsequent to that date. A combined boat and six-wheeled vehicle, the DUKW or "Duck" proved incredibly seaworthy, frequently able to traverse stormy seas without sinking, and moving at 6.4 mph in the water or up to 50 mph on a road.

The Pacific in 1943

The Guadalcanal landings represented the first of 39 opposed landings in the Pacific involving US forces of regimental strength or greater. Many other, smaller landings also occurred, as raids, diversions, or to carry out limited objectives. In mid-1943, the Americans tackled the New Georgia Group, a cluster of twelve large islands and numerous small islands that hosted an important 4,700-foot long Japanese airstrip.

This section of the Solomon Islands campaign, christened Operation Toenails, began on June 30, 1943. The initial landings on Rendova went unopposed in some cases, while at Rendova Harbor, the Japanese put up some resistance, including attacks by fighter aircraft and bombers. The American destroyers systematically shelled Japanese artillery and machine gun positions, however, and American air cover shot down many Japanese aircraft, preventing significant damage from air attack. The deep, liquid mud at the landing site proved an impediment nearly equaling the Japanese, ruining a considerable amount of supplies and swallowing a bulldozer whole.

The main assaulting troops, mostly men of 43rd Infantry Division, put ashore on New Georgia itself during the July 2nd to July 4th period. Heavy seas, stormy weather, and torrential rain made moving into position as well as landing a highly unpleasant experience. Once again, the men met no Japanese on the beach, though an abortive Japanese aerial attack alarmed the Americans while inflicting only trivial damage.

The landings on New Georgia, however, proved to be the easiest moment of the battle. The Japanese resisted with their usual fanaticism, and the Americans advanced through constant heavy rain over extremely broken terrain filled with jungle foliage, mud at the bottom of ravines, and knife-sharp coral boulders. Similar hard fighting occurred on the other islands of the group, and in one case Japanese dive-bombers succeeded in destroying an LST and killing 8 of the Americans aboard. By October 6th, 1943 the Americans completed their occupation of the New Georgia group.

The process of learning about amphibious operations, discovering the best use of new landing craft variants, and refining tactics as much as the chaos of combat allowed never ended during the course of the war. Additionally, each landing presented its own unique challenges and circumstances, caused by every conceivable factor from weather and details of terrain, to the personalities of opposing commanders, the exact forces available to each side, and chance or luck.

Following the successful conquest of New Georgia, the Americans' amphibious forces closed in on the island of Bougainville, a 125-mile long island mingling incredible tropical beauty such as huge, lush flowers and immense, colorful butterflies with hellish crocodile-infested swamps and legions of disease-bearing biting insects. Strong Japanese forces defended this location in the Solomon group, so the Americans and New Zealanders decided on heavy diversionary attacks to draw off some of the defenders.

As one of these large-scale diversions, joint American and New Zealand forces launched an amphibious assault on the Treasury Islands, code-named "Operation Goodtime." Using early LCIs with wooden hulls that offered little protection other than visual cover from enemy fire, the men came under heavy Japanese attack as their landing craft maneuvered toward the beach. One of the men, Peter Renshaw, left an account: "Fire from the shore began to crackle around the boat as we circled around before starting our run for shore. We could see a line of hills ahead as the boat picked up speed and began its run in to the beach. [...] Bullets whistled all around as the boat slowed to slam up on the shore [...]. It was too late to do anything but think about the job we had all been trained to do. The noise was deafening as the fire from the Jap guns and ours intermingled. [...] Then our mortars started to fire putting up a steady barrage ahead of the rifle companies." (Newell, 2012, 101-102).

During this attack, two of the new LCI(L) gunboats moved close inshore to fire at the Japanese defenders. Armed with a single 3-inch gun as well as an array of 20mm and 40mm cannons, these craft operated under the control of crews who had not yet had any rehearsal in the use of their vessels. The men performed their task with vigor, blowing apart a Japanese twin 40mm gun, destroying a bunker, and silencing several Japanese machine gun nests. However, the lack of rehearsal caused one of the gunboats to continue firing well after it should have stopped, pinning down its own troops on the left flank of the beachhead with streams of 20mm and 40mm shells. Eventually, the order to cease fire reached the LCI(L), enabling the men to move inland.

Rather than establishing a perimeter, the heavy fire of the Japanese defenders forced the New Zealand and American troops to move inland immediately to outflank the Japanese positions. Pounding the jungle ahead of them with mortar fire, the troops leapfrogged forward, eventually driving the Japanese back and clearing the way for subsequent waves to land with far less incoming fire. The landing illustrated how improvisation and flexibility proved key to handling the individual hazards of specific amphibious landings.

On November 1, 1943, the assault on Bougainville began with landings at Cape Torokina and the adjacent Puruata Island. Under the hot morning sun of the equatorial seas, Marines scrambled down cargo nets hung over the sides of their transports and into scores of landing craft assigned to carry them ashore to twelve designated assault beaches on Cape Torokina. A preliminary bombardment slammed the green tropical coastline with hundreds of heavy shells, while 8,000 men of the first wave prepared for a run to shore which ranged anywhere from 3,000-5,000 yards.

Hundreds of landing craft set off punctually through the characteristically heavy surf near the Bougainville coast. Before the day was out, a combination of strong surf and steep shores would strand 22 LCMs and 64 LCVPs, though the Americans recovered, repaired, and reused them in time.

As the landing craft approached the shore, the crash of a single artillery piece rang out, and one of the LCVPs blew apart as a 75mm HE shell tore it to pieces. Dead, dying, and unharmed Marines alike spilled into the water. A second shell ripped into another craft, followed by two more, shattering and killing both lieutenants on board, Byron Kirk and Harris Shelton, along with 12 other Marines, while 14 more men suffered serious wounds. The LCVP plowed onto the beach nevertheless and the unwounded Marines leaped out onto the sand. Several men tried to take the LCVP back to the ship, but it promptly sank, drowning all but four of the wounded.

The 75mm gun occupied an extremely sturdy bunker built from coconut logs and sandbags, which had survived the preparatory bombardment with basically no damage. It was, in fact, part of a Japanese defense in depth on the ground commanding the landing beaches on Cape Torokina. 270 Japanese soldiers under Captain Ichikawa occupied three rows of bunkers, 15 in the first row, 8 in the second row, and 2 in the rear.

The Japanese sited these bunkers with great skill so that the rearward rows could sweep the bunkers in front of them, keeping assault troops at bay. In addition to the 75mm gun, the Japanese troops had no less than 50 heavy machine guns at their disposal, and they now opened fire on the 8,000 Marines approaching the beach.

The 75mm gun, fired with great accuracy, completely destroyed four landing craft and badly damaged 10 more, killing 70 Marines and wounding scores of others. Driven into a rage by the sight of his comrades dying, USMC Sergeant Robert Owens charged the artillery bunker head-on and forced his body in through the firing port. The Japanese, taken by surprise by the American bursting into their midst in such an unexpected fashion, firing his M1 Garand at point blank range, bolted out the rear entrance of the bunker. Four Marines who had moved to support Owens mowed the Japanese down as they emerged.

Unfortunately for Owens, his battle frenzy was such that he charged out the rear of the bunker over the bodies of the fallen Japanese and rushed the two bunkers covering the rear of the artillery bunker. The Japanese in the rearward bunkers opened fire with their machine guns, filling the courageous sergeant with bullets and killing him almost instantly.

Owens' sacrifice, however, silenced the 75mm gun and allowed the rest of the landing craft to reach the shore relatively undamaged. When the Marines investigated the bunker later, they discovered an unfired 75mm shell inside the breach block, mere moments from being launched into the guts of another LCVP when Owens interrupted by hurling himself through the firing port. The sergeant received a posthumous Medal of Honor.

Over the next two hours, a desperate battle ensued between the Japanese in their bunkers firing their machine guns at any Marine who showed himself, and Marines crawling around the defensive structures seeking any way to defeat them. Numerous small actions occurred as the Marines encountered other Japanese in slit trenches, battles decided at point blank range with rifles, pistols, hand grenades, and fighting knives.

Finally, Captain Frank "Shorty" Vogel and a band of his men moved from bunker to bunker, systematically destroying them with grenades and demolition charges. The last six bunkers proved somewhat harder to defeat, but in the late morning, the Marines rolled up 75mm artillery pieces of their own and fired directly into the pillboxes, finally annihilating them. The Marines counted 202 dead Japanese, though others of the 270 probably crawled off to die in the jungle. Not one of the Japanese surrendered.

The two companies of Marines landing on Puruata Island under Lieutenant Colonel Fred Beans encountered similarly stiff resistance, though on a more limited scale. PFC "Dutch" Doornbos described some of the action: "[T]here were casualties from rifle and mortar fire in almost every Higgins boat before we hit the beach. […] It took us only a few minutes to get organized and the two companies pushed inland […] just about then the Nippers made a banzai charge on our positions in the village. They threw everything they had at us except the kitchen sink. But the two companies in the village just mowed down the charging Nips. After that charge the Japs were finished on Puruata except for a few snipers and the like." (Walling, 2017, 158-159).

Japanese snipers continued to plague the Marines on Bougainville, often shooting a man and then shooting the corpsman who came to assist him. The Marines, however, had an answer ready

– the 24 German Shepherds and Doberman Pinschers of the 1st Marine Dog Platoon. These dogs sniffed out many snipers, enabling the Marines to kill them before they opened fire, since the Japanese preferred to wait for larger bodies of troops before risking their first shot in the hope of maximizing casualties.

Several dogs entered history for their particular valor and usefulness. One Doberman, named Rollo, accompanied his handler Russel Frederick as Frederick scouted ahead of a Marine patrol. Japanese in a pair of concealed bunkers opened fire suddenly and Frederick fell to the ground mortally wounded. The other Marines whistled to Rollo, hoping to recall him, but the dog refused to leave his master. Instead, he lay down alongside Frederick as if to guard him. The Japanese continued firing into the dying Frederick and also hit and killed Rollo.

Another dog, a German shepherd named Caesar, made his way back and forth between two separated Marine units numerous times in a single day, carrying vital messages which allowed the men, isolated in the jungle, to coordinate their actions. In this case, though fired on repeatedly by the Japanese, Caesar survived unharmed.

Sustaining heavy losses, the Japanese fled to the interior of Bougainville, allowing the Americans to build a major airstrip. A final series of mostly unopposed landings in March 1944 on the Green Islands finished the Solomon Islands campaign, isolating the remaining Japanese garrisons in the region from resupply and giving the Americans a significant springboard for the next phase of operations.

One of the key pieces of knowledge gained from the Solomons campaign consisted of the fact that bypassing Japanese strongpoints and then starving them out frequently produced better results than a direct attack. In short, the Americans learned that the best tactical choice for an amphibious assault frequently consisted of not making an assault at all. With their active and effective combat engineers, the "Seabees," the Americans could often construct a usable airfield of their own almost as quickly as they could return a Japanese airfield to working order after it sustained battle damage.

The American juggernaut moved forward across the Pacific from island to island as the war progressed. In many cases, even on occupied islands, the Marines managed to land unopposed, only to be attacked after dark by Japanese raiding parties. In one instance, on the island of Los Negros, the Japanese launched a dawn banzai charge which opened with a chorus of frantic screams and yells – and then, as a profoundly surreal finale, the Japanese soldiers began singing "Deep in the Heart of Texas" as they charged vainly to their deaths in a storm of Marine gunfire.

Also in 1943, the Americans began operations to take the Marshall Islands and the Gilbert Islands. This led to the famous Battle of Tarawa Atoll on November 20th to 23rd, 1943. This battle, which pitted the 2nd Marine Division and the 27th Infantry Division against 2,636 Japanese troops and 2,200 laborers, became one of the most brutally fought opposed landings, and witnessed the large-scale use of LVT-1 and LVT-2 tracked "alligators" by the Americans in their assault on Betio Island.

The Japanese arrayed 14 coastal defense guns in concrete bunkers, backed up by 40 artillery pieces in firing pits and nearly 500 pillboxes built from coconut logs. Keiji Shibizaki, commandant of the island, believed that the Americans would fail when the attacked this deadly, dug-in force.

On the first day of the amphibious assault, the Marines aimed for the three "Red Beaches" on the north side of the island, while attacks on "Green Beach" on Betio's western side began on the second day, November 21st. As the 125 amphibious tractors moved inshore, laden with men, the Japanese met them with a firestorm of artillery, mortar, machine gun, and small arms fire which smashed LVTs to pieces or plunged through their thin steel armor to wound and kill the men inside.

The armor plate provided full protection from rifle and machine gun bullets at long and medium range, but as the LVTs crawled across the exposed reef in the lagoon and approached the shore, these lesser projectiles also began to punch through to the interior. PFC Newman Baird described his own experience under this incessant Japanese fire: "They were knocking [LVTs] out left and right. A tractor'd get hit, stop, and burst into flames, with men jumping out like torches. […] I grabbed my carbine and an ammunition box and stepped over a couple of fellas lying there and put my hand on the side so's to roll over into the water. I didn't want to put my head up. The bullets were pouring at us like a sheet of rain." (Walling, 2017, 320).

Pinned down on the beaches, the Marines sheltered behind coconut log retaining walls along Betio's fringe. While the LVTs managed to cross the exposed reef and deposit their occupants onshore – at least if they survived the fatal gantlet of Japanese fire – the followup wave of LCVPs could not cross the reef. The men aboard them debarked 500 yards from the beach and waded all the way to shore through water lashed and churned by constant waves of Japanese machine gun and rifle bullets.

The Marines also attempted to deploy 14 Sherman M4A2 tanks and 36 M3A1 Stuart light tanks, only to have all four of their LCMs sunk near the reef. The surviving tanks rolled inshore through the shallow water, with men walking in front of them to warn them of underwater pits and craters. The Japanese targeted these guides and few survived more than a minute or two, but another man always proved willing to take their place.

A number of tanks reached the shore but found more difficulties awaiting them. With the ground carpeted in many places with writhing, wounded Marines, the tank crews did not wish to drive over their own injured comrades. The log retaining wall, which provided the infantry with welcome cover, proved a hindrance to the tanks until breached with explosives. The Japanese destroyed 12 of the 14 Shermans by nightfall on "D-Day."

The Marines held onto their slim beachheads through the night despite Japanese banzai charges, and on the following day more men poured ashore, many forced to wade across the reef and 500 yards of lagoon before reaching cover. Over the next several days, the Marines systematically reduced the defenses using pack howitzers, flamethrowers, grenades, and indomitable pluck. The Japanese exhausted their strength in futile nighttime banzai attacks. By the fourth day, only 17 Japanese survived to be taken prisoner, along with 129 laborers. 4,690 defenders died, while the Americans sustained 687 KIA.

The action at Tarawa proved essentially useless. While the Americans won, the island had no strategic significance and the men attacking it died for little military purpose when it could easily have been bypassed. It did, however, prove the absolute superiority of the tracked LVTs to the LCVPs, as well as highlighting the need for amphibious tanks.

The American island offensive carried on through 1944 and into 1945, retaking the islands the Japanese had added to their expanding empire just a few years before. Many amphibious assaults occurred during this steady drive in the direction of Japan itself, each inevitably heralded by the unusually excellent breakfast served to the troops before the attack, consisting of steak, eggs, fried potatoes, buttered toast, milk, and fruit juices.

The Americans deployed both amphibious tanks – "amtanks" – and amphibious tractors for their assault on the Marianas Islands of Guam, Tinian, and Saipan. The amtanks – LVT(A)-1 and LVT(A)-2 variants, with the "A" standing for "Armored" – featured thicker steel armor and 37mm guns in turrets. These "Water Buffaloes" formed the first waves onto the landing beaches due to their higher levels of protection, with ordinary LVT-1 and LVT-2 tractors forming later waves.

By this time, the American troops used in the assault had survived multiple landings – some of them even veterans of the slaughter on Tarawa – and no longer appeared as frightened late adolescents. Seasoned, battle-hardened, and confident, these formidable assault troops now carried their rifles in clear plastic waterproof cases and bore packed lunches of sandwiches to eat in the midst of the coming mayhem.

The Marines and U.S. Army troops landed in the teeth of Japanese machine gun and light artillery fire which brewed up some of their amtracks, then systematically cleared the thick jungle and numerous caves of the Marianas of Japanese troops. The Japanese killed most of their own civilians before or during their own suicides when defeat appeared inevitable, horrifying the Americans.

Iwo Jima

On February 23, 1945, one of the most famous photographs in American history was taken atop Mount Suribachi, as five American soldiers began to raise an American flag. The picture, which most Americans are instantly familiar with, has come to symbolize the strength and sacrifice of America's armed forces, and though many realize it was taken during the Battle of Iwo Jima, much of the actual battle and the context of the picture itself have been overshadowed.

The Battle of Iwo Jima, code name "Operation Detachment," is more of a misnomer than anything. It was fought as part of a large American invasion directed by steps toward the Japanese mainland, and it was more like a siege that lasted 36 days from February-March 1945, with non-stop fighting every minute. In fact, the iconic flag-raising photo was taken just four days into the battle, and as that picture suggests, the battle was not a pristine tactical event but an unceasing horror with no haven for protection. As veteran and author James F. Christ put it in the foreword of his exhaustive study of the action, "it is carnage…that is what Iwo was…the Gettysburg of the Pacific." Iwo Jima defined the classical amphibious assault of the World War II era, as much as the Normandy invasion did, but it came later in the war. In Europe, the Battle of the Bulge had already been won, and German forces would surrender in early May. However, the Japanese Empire was still at a considerable level of strength and state of resolve, and an essential offensive, grinding from island to island with naval unit to naval unit and air to air was met with maniacal resistance by the enemy.

When Admiral Chester Nimitz was directed to capture an island in the Bonin group, Iwo Jima stood out for its importance in making progress against the mainland, with three airfields that would allow American air forces to attack the Japanese mainland. But the Japanese were also well aware of how important Iwo Jima was, and they fought desperately in bunkers and tunnels that required the Americans to carefully clear them out gradually. Less than 5% of the Japanese soldiers on Iwo Jima were taken alive, and American casualties were estimated at 26,000, with 6,800 killed or captured. A month later at Okinawa, which lasted from April-June, the Americans suffered an estimated 62,000 casualties, with 12,000 Americans killed or captured. These deadly campaigns came after widely-held predictions that taking these islands would amount to no more than a brief footnote in the overall theater. However, the national character of the Empire was equally misunderstood. Following the month of Iwo Jima, "commentator after commentator in the Anglo-American camp agreed that the Japanese were more despised than the Germans…uncommonly treacherous and savage…alluding to their remarkable tenacity…refused to give up any territory and incurred thousands of losses daily without any possibility of surrender." The fighting went a long way toward swaying the beliefs of American military advisors that invading Japan itself would cause millions of casualties, which ultimately helped induce President Truman to use the atomic bombs on Hiroshima and Nagasaki.

At 2:00 a.m. on the 19th of February, battleship guns announced the beginning of the Iwo Jima offensive, also called D-Day like its more famous European counterpart. Soon after, over 100 bombers assaulted the island, followed by more bombs dropped by carrier aircraft. At 8:59 a.m., a minute ahead of schedule, the first of 30,000 men from the 3rd, 4th and 5th Marines began to land, and they would be followed by 40,000 more later in the day. The first aim was to neutralize and capture Mount Suribachi, and though these landing forces weren't fought on the beach by Japanese infantry, they had to deal with heavy artillery being fired at them by well-hidden units. The Japanese would open the steel doors to let their artillery pieces fire, close the door while reloading, and fire again. The Japanese also wisely waited for as many Marines as possible to land on the beach, thus offering more targets for the artillery.

Thanks to the Japanese strategy of offering light resistance (at least from their infantry), the Marines quickly found their landing zones congested, so much so that the 21st Marine regiment was boated and prepared to land but couldn't due to lack of space. With space so limited, some troops re-embarked onto their respective ships and landed later in the afternoon. When the Marines who landed encountered no Japanese forces, they mistakenly thought most of them had been killed in the bombardment. In fact, the Japanese were merely waiting for their approach, and the first lines of Marines that did approach on the 19th were quickly mowed down by machine gun fire once they got within range of the hidden Japanese positions.

Marines burrowing in on the beach

While the Marines had to contend with artillery on Mount Suribachi, important naval actions took place around the area and mitigated the potential damage. On February 18, the U.S. carrier *Enterprise* task groups 58.5, 58.4 and 58.1 separated from the main group, and headed for a refueling rendezvous to the southwest of Iwo Jima. The next morning (D-Day for the Marines), *Enterprise* refueled and set course 60 miles northwest of Iwo Jima. *Enterprise's* primary responsibility on the 19th was to protect amphibious forces from air attacks, and at 1630, she launched six Night Air Group 90 Hellcats to cover the forces at dusk. Two hours later, four VF (N)-90 fighters encountered eight interceptions, but most of the Japanese planes turned away and declined to engage. Before 1930, an enemy "Helen" (twin-engine heavy bomber) was knocked out of the sky (or as the Navy and Air Force was fond of saying, "they splashed it.").

On the 20th, the Marines advanced from the south of Mount Suribachi, north of the airfield, and satchel charges and flame throwers were used to reach entrenched Japanese forces on the mountain, all while cruisers and destroyers bombarded Japanese positions. Furthermore, ravines were set with gasoline fires to force the enemy out of entrenched positions. However, the elaborate tunnels dug by the Japanese allowed their men to flee further inward from the use of fire instead of being smoked out, and when the attacks would stop, the Japanese defenders could simply move right back into position. Another problem hampering the Marines was that the use of tanks in this theater of operations had a major disadvantage; a Sherman tank was difficult to disable, often requiring that Japanese attackers come out in the open, but the terrain throughout most of the island was not suited for armored movement.

A Sherman tank equipped with a flame-thrower attacks Japanese positions on Iwo Jima

Supplies landing at Iwo Jima

While the Marines inched their way toward Mount Suribachi and the airfield on the southern end of Iwo Jima, the navy was attempting to prevent attacks by Japanese planes taking off from nearby islands. After 0900 on the 21st of February, the *Enterprise* and the *Saratoga* CV-3 split up. *Saratoga* and her three escort destroyers went to join Task Group 52.2, Rear Admiral Calvin Durgin's forces of escort carriers to the northeast of Iwo Jima. *Saratoga* operated in tandem with *Lexington* CV-16 and *Hancock* CV-19. "Saratoga was now 'Queen of the Jeeps" (escort carriers), but her reign was short-lived."[1] Before 1600, she picked up a large "bogey" on radar that turned out to be a mass of 20-25 planes at a distance of approximately 75 miles. They were first identified as friendly due to the belief that American air patrols were returning, but when planes were sent aloft to confirm it, they shot down two Zeroes. The body of enemy planes emerged from the low fog and descended on *Saratoga*, which took three direct hits from the planes' bombs, while two enemy planes fell off the starboard side and one crashed directly into the flight deck. The crew fought the fires for 90 minutes as the carrier sped up to 25 knots, but a second attack began four hours later and *Saratoga* was targeted by five suicide planes. In the attack, the *Saratoga* was badly damaged, and the USS *Bismarck Sea* was sunk, making it the last carrier to sink during World War II.

---

[1] USS Enterprise: 1945 Iwo Jima

By the last day of February, the third airfield was occupied by Marines, but the surrounding hills were still held by the Japanese. Soon after, Marines assaulted the hills, 362A and 382, successfully taking and holding them by the 1st of March. The following night, an after-dusk attack was staged by Marines on Hill 362A, but the hill would not be secured until the 8th of March. On March 4th, a damaged B-29 landed on the island during the fighting, an important sign that Marines were sufficiently in control of the airfield to make landings possible. The first P-51s would arrive at the island as air support for Marines by March 6th, and Task Force 58 was relieved in preparation for a subsequent assault against Okinawa.

By the end of the first week of March, the southern airfield was fully operational for the Americans, and evacuation of the wounded proceeded without interruption. Since Iwo Jima was interconnected with so many simultaneous actions proceeding in the South Pacific, the bombing of the airfields in Chichi Jima was of great parallel importance, and attacks on Paulus and Yap in the western Carolines ensured that the strategic air importance of Iwo Jima would not simply be transferred to another site by the Japanese. Somewhat symbolically, of all the flag-raisings on Suribachi, the final one was hoisted by the U.S. Combat Team 28 on March 14, 1945, near the end of the conflict.

Over the course of March, the Japanese continued desperately attacking, including mounting a counterattack on the 23rd and 24th Marine Regiments, but that assault was stopped by artillery, and 650 of the enemy were killed. Resistance continued throughout the following days as Japanese units repeatedly penetrated American lines in attempts to sever communication, but the defense had just about reached its last gasp. The final Japanese resistance was overcome at Kitano Point on March 25th, and the last Japanese unit to attempt a penetration of the American lines was allegedly led by Kuribayashi himself. The result of that action left 250 more Japanese dead, including Kuribayashi. At 8:00 a.m. on March 26, the island was declared secure, although a lengthy time would go by before final resistance was rooted out of the caves. Either way, the 147th U.S. Army Infantry arrived for garrison duty on Iwo Jima by March 20 and would have full control of the island by the 4th of April. By April 7, 100 P-51s were able to land on the island and subsequently escort a B-29 bombing raid against the Japanese mainland. It would be incorrect to assume that once the island came under American control, the fighting stopped or the environment became safe. It was clearly operational, but not necessarily safe, and casualties were suffered through the last day of American occupation.

The island of Iwo Jima remained under American control for several years even after the war, until it was eventually returned to the Japanese in 1968. In the last months of the war, the aircraft carrier USS *Iwo Jima* was under construction at Newport News, Virginia, but she was canceled on August 12, 1945 and her partial hull was scrapped. Her namesake, however, was launched from Bremerton, Washington in 1960 and commissioned in 1961. Today, no civilians are allowed on the island, and the Japanese operate a naval base there. American carriers still use it for landing training, and nuclear weapons are said to have been located at one time or another on

Iwo Jima, Ton Chichi, Okinawa and other Japanese sites.

Final casualties for the entire Iwo Jima offensive have been estimated at 6,821 American dead and 19,189 wounded, compared to 20,000 Japanese dead and 1,083 wounded and/or captured. Clearly, fighting to the death and committing suicide were prevalent among the Japanese ranks. In this strategy of sacrifice, the Japanese remained true to their word, and of the few prisoners taken, many were conscripted Korean laborers. It has even been estimated that up to 6,000 Japanese fighters are still entombed within the network of caves.

Okinawa

Near the end of 1944, as Allied forces were pushing across the Pacific and edging ever closer to Japan, plans were drawn up to invade the Ryuku islands, the most prominent of them being Okinawa. Military planners anticipated that an amphibious campaign would last a week, but instead of facing 60,000 Japanese defenders as estimated, there were closer to 120,000 on the island at the beginning of the campaign in April 1945. The Battle of Okinawa was the largest amphibious operation in the Pacific theater, and it would last nearly 3 months and wind up being the fiercest in the Pacific theater during the war, with nearly 60,000 American casualties and over 100,000 Japanese soldiers killed. In addition, the battle resulted in an estimated 40,000-150,000 Japanese civilian casualties.

Okinawa witnessed every conceivable horror of war both on land and at sea. American ground forces on Okinawa had to deal with bad weather (including a typhoon), anti-tank moats, barbed wire, mines, caves, underground tunnel networks, and fanatical Japanese soldiers who were willing to use human shields while fighting to the death. Allied naval forces supporting the amphibious invasion had to contend with Japan's notorious kamikazes, suicide pilots who terrorized sailors as they frantically tried to shoot down the Japanese planes before they could hit Allied ships. As one sailor aboard the USS *Miami* recalled, "They came in swarms from all directions. The barrels of our ship's guns got so hot we had to use firehoses to cool them down." As *The Marine Corps Gazette* noted, "More mental health issues arose from the Battle of Okinawa than any other battle in the Pacific during World War II. The constant bombardment from artillery and mortars coupled with the high casualty rates led to a great deal of men coming down with combat fatigue. Additionally the rains caused mud that prevented tanks from moving and tracks from pulling out the dead, forcing Marines (who pride themselves on burying their dead in a proper and honorable manner) to leave their comrades where they lay. This, coupled with thousands of bodies both friend and foe littering the entire island, created a scent you could nearly taste. Morale was dangerously low by the month of May and the state of discipline on a moral basis had a new low barometer for acceptable behavior. The ruthless atrocities by the Japanese throughout the war had already brought on an altered behavior (deemed so by traditional standards) by many Americans resulting in the desecration of Japanese remains, but the Japanese tactic of using the Okinawan people as human shields brought about a new aspect of terror and torment to the psychological capacity of the Americans."

Given the horrific nature of the combat, and the fact that it was incessant for several weeks, it's no surprise that Okinawa had a profound psychological effect on the men who fought, but it also greatly influenced the thinking of military leaders who were planning subsequent campaigns, including a potential invasion of the Japanese mainland. The fighting at places like Iwo Jima and Okinawa went a long way toward swaying the beliefs of American military advisors that invading Japan itself would cause millions of casualties, which ultimately helped compel President Truman to use the atomic bombs on Hiroshima and Nagasaki in an effort to end the war before having to attempt such an invasion.

As Allied troops began the campaign, they quickly took the Kerama islands, which Japan had failed to fortify because they did not believe the islands possessed sufficient importance to be targeted by an American attack. American forces occupied all of the islands by March 29th, while the British Task Force 57 reached its position for the attack on Okinawa on March 26th. As American naval vessels moved on Okinawa, the last task before the attack was to clear the waters off the coast of mines. In the last week of March, 5,182 tons of shells were fired at the Ryukyus to soften their defenses. The next part of the plan would involve landing ground troops on Okinawa.

Allied soldiers landing on the Kerama islands.

The ground invasion was set to begin on April 1, 1945, and on that day, over 1,300 ships were involved in landing soldiers on the island. American forces had gained plenty of experience in amphibious landings over the past two years, but unlike at Guadalcanal or the Marianas, the Japanese did not contest the beach areas, allowing 60,000 troops to come ashore by the end of the first day. As they moved toward Okinawa's two main airfields, they experienced little resistance and quickly captured them.

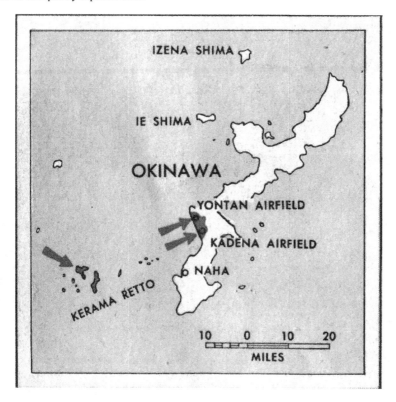

The invasion plan on April 1.

The USS *Idaho* shelling Okinawa on April 1.

Marines coming ashore on April 1.

American forces moving on the beaches of Okinawa, April 1.

Unlike American ground troops on day 1 of the assault, naval forces positioned off the coast were attacked. Admiral Spruance's flagship, the *Indianapolis*, as well as the battleship *West Virginia*, two transports, and one landing ship were all hit by suicide attacks. The British carrier *Indefatigable* was also hit by a kamikaze plane, but it remained able to continue launching and recovering planes. As the first day came to an end, casualties were much lighter than military estimates had assumed, and it was a surprise that American forces had captured the airfields so quickly. However, Allied officials understood that the Japanese would not simply capitulate, especially not on an island so close to the home islands.

Ahead of the invasion of Okinawa, the Japanese commander at Okinawa, Lieutenant General Ushijima of the 32nd Army, positioned his troops to execute the commands that had been given to him: to hold Okinawa until the end and exact as heavy a price as possible on the Allied forces invading the island. The 32nd Army had been weakened when its 9th Division was sent to Formosa, but they still possessed an important artillery arsenal greater than any the Americans had faced in the Pacific so far. In fact, Ushijima's decision not to contest Okinawa's beaches probably stemmed from his desire to keep his artillery from being attacked by American warplanes and naval guns. Instead, he positioned them inland where they would be safer, a similar tactic to the one the Japanese used at Iwo Jima. Ushijima also conceded the airfields as indefensible and opted to position his troops in fortifications around the island.

Ushijima

A picture of Japanese commanders on Okinawa in February 1945. (1) Admiral Minoru Ota, (2) Lt. Gen. Mitsuru Ushijima, (3) Lt. Gen. Isamu Cho, (4) Col. Hitoshi Kanayama, (5) Col. Kikuji Hongo, and (6) Col. Hiromichi Yahara.

On the second day of their attack, the invading forces altered the plan due to the ease with which they had captured the airfields. Instead of first attacking the southern portion of the island before moving to the north, American troops would now simultaneously take both areas of the island. From the beginning of their advances, however, both thrusts, made up of Lieutenant General Simon Bolivar Buckner, Jr.'s Tenth Army (moving north) and Major General John R. Hodge's XXIV Corps (moving south), began to encounter resistance in the form of camouflaged Japanese positions surrounded by minefields.

Hodge

Bolivar, Jr.

Spruance, Nimitz, and Buckner

On Hodge's drive south, the 7th Division, which was positioned along the left flank, fell behind the 96th Division when they were engaged by Japanese forces positioned along a ridge parallel to the coastline near the town of Kuba. After an aerial bombardment of the Japanese position, the 7th Division engaged in a frontal assault that was turned back by the Japanese units. A second aerial bombardment was followed by a second frontal assault, but that attack also failed. On their third attempt, the men of the 7th Division again proceeded with a frontal assault, but this time the division's Company C broke off and flanked the Japanese position. The Japanese were completely surprised by this maneuver, and Japanese soldiers defending the ridge were wiped out when Company C brought the brunt of their grenades and flamethrowers on them. This would establish a pattern in American engagement with Japanese troops on Okinawa, because while the Japanese were very skilled at defending against a frontal assault, they were constantly unable to cope with flanking maneuvers. After gaining the sightline of the ridge, American reconnaissance could start to determine the positions of Japanese forces in the defensive zone around the town of Shuri (Frank, p. 70).

At the end of May, American forces had been on Okinawa for two months, and they had killed over 62,000 Japanese soldiers, with another 9,500 estimated as killed. About 8,000 of these deaths had occurred in northern Okinawa, with the rest occurring in southern Okinawa. The Americans had also suffered heavy casualties, with the III Amphibious Corps and XXIV Corps suffering 26,044 casualties. The Marines had suffered 6,315 casualties, while the army had 7,762 casualties, but even with these casualties, the ratio of Americans killed to Japanese killed was still roughly 1:10 (Gow, p.166-167). Added to the casualty numbers were issues of exhaustion; over 61 days of fighting, the 96th Division had fought for 50 days, the 7th Division had fought for 49 days, and the 77th Division fought for 32 days.

On June 22, the Battle of Okinawa officially concluded as American troops finally controlled the entire island, but Okinawa has remained an endless source of both fascination and controversy. One of the most notable aspects of the battle was the Japanese's determination to fight to the death, but they also forced civilians into fighting and even forced civilians to commit mass suicide when the end was near. A recent documentary has asserted "there were two types of orders for 'honorable deaths' - one for residents to kill each other and the other for the military to kill all residents." As a result, it's believed that over 100,000 civilians may have been killed, a number made all the more difficult to estimate due to the fact that an untold number evacuated into caves and were entombed in them when American soldiers sealed them as they advanced in order to protect themselves. American troops also used flamethrowers to smoke the Japanese out of caves, and in the process, it was impossible to distinguish civilians from soldiers.

An American Marine using a flamethrower on a Japanese cave.

Most importantly, the Battle of Okinawa was so ruthless that it convinced Allied leaders that the invasion of Japan would be an absolute bloodbath for all sides. American military officials estimated that there would be upwards of a million Allied casualties if they had to invade the Japanese mainland, and if they were successful, Japan would suffer tens of millions of casualties in the process. As the Battle of Okinawa was about to finish, America's secret Manhattan Project was on the brink of its final goal: a successful detonation of a nuclear device. On July 16, 1945, the first detonation of a nuclear device took place in Alamogordo, New Mexico.

North Africa

The Western Allies made use of amphibious landings in both the North African theater as well, using the same landing craft, for the most part, as those that saw service in the Pacific. Rather than dozens of landings on tiny islands scattered across the vastness of the world's largest ocean, however, the amphibious operations against the Germans landed on continental coasts.

This difference translated to both more options for landing sites (with hundreds, if not thousands, of miles of coast to choose from) and the necessity for massive amphibious assaults. While the attackers enjoyed the advantage of choosing from many possible landing sites, greatly increasing the odds of surprise, the defenders could concentrate large forces rapidly at the landing site, a very different situation from the Pacific. Strategic landings, therefore, needed to be large enough to survive potential divisional-sized or even corps-sized counterattacks from the Wehrmacht.

The first landing, Operation Torch, aimed at putting a joint American and British/Commonwealth force ashore in Vichy French territory in North Africa in late 1942. The Allies correctly identified the French zone as the weakest link, since the Vichy French had little desire to fight the British, the Free French, or the Americans. From there, the forces could move east to engage the beleaguered Afrika Korps of Field Marshal Erwin Rommel, known as the "Desert Fox."

The Allies contacted the Vichy French through diplomatic and informal channels, attempting to prompt them to switch sides or at least stand down and not oppose the landings. These negotiations largely came to nothing, however.

The Operation Torch landings in November 1942 took place in three separate areas hundreds of miles apart, as the troops carried by the Eastern, Central, and Western Task Forces came ashore. The landings included both day and night assaults, and met some resistance from the Vichy French, including strafing and bombing attacks, artillery fire, and in some cases infantry fire as well, though delivered in a half-hearted fashion.

The high surf along the coasts proved to be more of a hazard than the French in many instances. American Lieutenant Jack Elliott described a landing which provided a microcosm of the conditions encountered in many places along the North African coast: "The rapidly rising and falling tide in the small river connecting Fedala and the airport at Port Lyautey, estimated at eleven feet, and the crashing combers along the coastal areas […] created a combined hazard the wrecked many of our landing craft and caused the drowning deaths of an inordinate number of troops." (Walling, 2017, 82).

American soldiers landing during Operation Torch

Despite these difficulties and desultory but occasional lethal French resistance, the American, British, and Commonwealth troops carried out their far-flung landings successfully for the most part. The French surrendered piecemeal, firing only a few shots before giving up in some areas and keeping up a relatively brisk resistance before surrendering in others.

The Allied forces had gotten ashore in North Africa, and over the following few months they defeated Rommel's now considerably outnumbered Afrika Korps. Those Germans who could escaped to Sicily or Italy, where the Allies would soon follow them, opening up a new front on the European continent.

Sicily

The Anglo-American strategic conference held at Casablanca between January 14th and 24th, 1943, decided the course of the war during that year. The American negotiators at the Anfa Hotel proposed a modest landing in France to establish a beachhead for later operations. The British, by contrast, preferred Sicily, and rapidly prevailed in the debate: "'If I had written down before I came what I hoped the conclusions would be,' one British planner noted, 'I could never have written anything so sweeping, so comprehensive, and so favourable to our ideas.' Wedemeyer, the chief [American] army planner at Casablanca, bluntly concluded 'that we lost our shirts... One might say that we came, we listened, and we were conquered.'" (Stoler, 2000, 103).

The Americans' plan, developed by Dwight D. Eisenhower with notable skill and speed, bore the codename Operation Roundup. This scheme, eventually used as the basis for developing Operation Overlord (the D-Day landings), envisioned setting 48 divisions ashore in France during spring of 1943, supported by over 5,000 aircraft.

A picture of General Eisenhower in North Africa with (foreground, left to right): Air Chief Marshal Sir Arthur Tedder, General Sir Harold R. L. G. Alexander, Admiral Sir Andrew B. Cunningham, and (top row): Mr. Harold Macmillan, Major General W. Bedell Smith, and unidentified British officers.

However, the material strength needed to carry out a plan of this scale did not exist at that stage of the war. The Anglo-Americans lacked sufficient ships in early 1943 to transport a force so large despite the United States' remarkable industrial output, while aircraft production also lagged behind the necessary totals. Supplying the force after landing would likely have proven a logistical impossibility. Furthermore, the Luftwaffe still controlled European skies, not yet decimated by America's lethal P-51 Mustangs and other high quality, well piloted, and numerous aircraft of the late war period.

The British, in exchange for an American agreement to land in Sicily rather than their preferred target of France, offered the concession of strengthening their military presence in Burma, leading to the eventual deployment of over a million soldiers against the southwestern frontier of the Empire of Japan. The English also noted the strategic advantages gained by opening the Mediterranean route to Lend-Lease shipments to the Soviet Union, a forecast revealed as accurate by the result.

The Americans and British each offered a unique contribution to the preparations for Operation

Husky, the hugest seaborne landing then attempted in the history of warfare. Superior quality landing craft and pontoons proved the indispensable element provided by the United States. The backbone of the landings, without which moving nearly 200,000 men ashore rapidly would have proven impossible, consisted of the DUKW.

Predictably but aptly dubbed the "Duck," the DUKW amphibious transport rolled off General Motors Corporation (GMC) assembly lines in thousands between 1942 and 1945, eventually totaling over 21,000 vehicles. DUKWs, based on a heavily modified 2.5-ton truck chassis, showed extraordinary seaworthiness, surviving 20-foot waves kicked up by 70 mph winds to deliver troops safely to the beach in some instances. Successful deployment of Allied forces through the violent surf present during the initial Husky landings would have been impracticable without the superb American landing craft.

The Duck

The other vital American contribution came from the Navy's Construction Battalions, or Seabees: "Navy engineers [...] countered with Project GOLDRUSH: a floating pontoon that could be towed or carried in sections on the LSTs, then bolted together to form an articulated bridge across the water gap from sandbar to beach. Tests in Narragansett Bay had proved the bridge could bear a Sherman tank." (Atkinson, 2007, 60).

Allied vehicle and artillery strength also reached impressive totals. One thousand eight hundred pieces of field artillery, 600 tanks, and 14,000 other vehicles – ranging from armored cars to trucks, Jeeps, and halftracks – came ashore with the landing force. The Americans fielded most of these vehicles; the British complained of their own mobility-limiting lack of vehicular support and relatively weak tank forces, while the Canadians made use of American-built M1 tanks alongside British and Canadian vehicles.

This gigantic force would move ashore carried or supported by 2,590 ships. 1,839 of these consisted of shipborne landing craft providing transport from the troopships to the beach; of these, the American DUKW (an amphibious troop transport) and LST (Landing Ship Tank, for tanks and other vehicles) proved instrumental in the landing's success. 1,670 combat aircraft and 835 transport and support aircraft offered air support and delivered paratroopers to the Sicilian operation. As more reinforcements arrived, Allied troop numbers eventually swelled to 467,000 men.

Notable British aircraft included the hard-hitting Supermarine Spitfire, scourge of the Luftwaffe during the Battle of Britain, and the Hawker Hurricane, an aging but still useful design. The Americans contributed B-17 and B-24 bombers, C-47 transport aircraft, and P-38 Lightnings, the last of which soon established a formidable reputation among German soldiers subjected to their relentless strafing.

At the moment that the first British and American boots thudded into the sand of Sicily's southern beaches, around 230,000 Italians and 40,000 Germans garrisoned the island. Axis troop totals remained vague and uncertain throughout the struggle, as some units arrived as reinforcements at the same time as others withdrew to the Italian mainland. The highest Wehrmacht troop total reached an estimated 65,000, while the Italians never numbered more than a quarter million men.

The day before the invasion fleet launched, July 8th, 1943, most of the men already waited aboard the ships. Ominously – though most of the men lacked the meteorological knowledge to spot the coming trouble – the sea lay smooth and motionless as a mirror under a blast furnace sun. Confined below decks in case Axis reconnaissance aircraft passed over, the men sweltered in stifling conditions, checking their gear or writing letters.

Lieutenant Commander Richard C. Steere, an MIT meteorologist known for such uncannily accurate forecasts that Patton called him "Commander Houdini," reported that a polar front would produce a windstorm on the following day, July 9th, while the fleet sailed for Sicily. In response to Patton's queries, Steere also confidently predicted the windstorm's cessation by "D-Day," July 10th. He also suggested that Sicily itself, blocking the northern gale, would reduce wave heights in its lee.

Early on the morning of the 9th, the huge armada set sail across the Mediterranean towards Sicily. Nearly 3,000 vessels, including flat-bottomed LSIs (Landing Ship Infantry) and LSTs (Landing Ship Tank) alongside escorting destroyers and numerous other craft, left their North

African berths and set out across the darkened Mediterranean. Calm prevailed for a few hours, but then the windstorm Steere predicted swept in from the northwest. The sea turned an ominous green color and gathered itself into hurrying mountains of sliding, battering water topped with wild crests of foam. At around noon, when the armada drew parallel with Malta, the gale achieved extraordinary violence, with winds of 35 miles per hour (Beaufort scale 7) and 16 foot wave heights reported.

As the ships pitched and tossed alarmingly on the tumultuous sea, filled with frightened, vomiting soldiers, Patton called for Steere and asked him whether the invasion could go ahead. Steere boldly stuck to his prediction that the winds would cease before the next day. The only members of the expedition seemingly unperturbed by the "Mussolini wind," as the soldiers colorfully dubbed their airy tormenter, were the pack donkeys: "'Ship rolled thirty degrees and pitched fifteen,' a naval officer recorded. 'Donkeys were unconcerned, and seemed to enjoy their hay splashed with salt water.'" (Atkinson, 2007, 65).

At around the time Patton queried Steere about the weather forecast, the commander of the Canadian contingent received information that a highly placed spy in Mussolini's government claimed a remote-detonated minefield lay exactly in his assigned path. Unwilling to turn back but nervous, the commander asked Simonds his opinion of the matter. The cold, aloof Canadian officer considered it briefly before dismissing the report as false, as indeed it was. Even Simonds, however, appeared nervous in the face of the worsening gale, warily watching the huge waves crash against the ship.

The ships drew close to Sicily after nightfall on the 9th, with an early morning landing scheduled for Saturday, July 10th, 1943. At 9:00 p.m. that night, the winds dropped sharply, seemingly vindicating Steere's predictions, and the men prepared to go ashore in an almost cheerful mood. However, when the invasion armada approached within eight miles of the Sicilian coast, the "Mussolini wind" increased again suddenly, growing even more violent than during the day.

"Commander Houdini's" prediction had been incorrect this time, but the attack went ahead anyway. Bombers struck the shore defenses shortly before the ships came into range, lighting up the northern horizon with brilliant flashes of light, followed by a wavering glow from incinerated crop fields. Soon the defenders on the shore at the chosen points of attack heard, above the sound of the wind and ocean, a deep rolling, throbbing sound from thousands of ship engines straining against the gale-driven waters.

A visually spectacular, lethally violent pageant began at 2:45 a.m. on July 10th. Moving ahead of the troop ships, Royal Navy destroyers moved inshore, using gigantic spotlights to sweep the Sicilian coastline and pick out targets for their powerful guns. The Luftwaffe and Italian air forces sprang into action, dropping searingly bright magnesium flares on parachutes to illuminate the ocean for miles and braving a storm of flak to strafe, bomb, and dive-bomb the approaching vessels. An eccentric British anti-aircraft officer, Derrick Leverton, who also worked as an undertaker and commanded his battery wearing a helmet, blue swimming trunks, and sandals due to the heat, described the approach to Sicily's shore at H-Hour: "With flares, searchlights and blazing fires, plus the vivid chromatic effects of bomb bursts and shell explosions, all of Sicily so far as the eye could reach was like nothing in the world so much as a huge pyrotechnical show." (Macintyre, 2010, 241). Leverton, an incorrigible optimist despite his profession and his disconcerting habit of referring to trenches and foxholes as "graves," continued to enjoy the scenes immensely, even expressing gratitude for a splash of cool seawater thrown up refreshingly by a near miss from a Stuka dive-bomber.

Even as the Allied landing craft undertook the final push towards the Sicilian coast, other Anglo-American soldiers already occupied a few scraps of Sicily's territory. The participants in two airborne insertions named "Husky 1" and "Ladbroke" suffered disastrously from poor planning and execution of the plan, but nevertheless, they caused disproportionate confusion and demoralization in the Italian and even some of the German troops, who believed them far more numerous than they were.

3,405 paratroopers from the 505th Parachute Infantry Regiment, supplemented by the 3/504th, set out under the command of Colonel James Gavin in 226 C-47 transports. Separated and confused by the darkness and the high winds, the aircraft dropped the paratroopers in a haphazard manner, some landing in the British sector and the rest scattered in small groups across the countryside. A few units managed to take their objectives, mostly minor bridges and road junctions, but most ended up lost. These men attacked Italian targets of opportunity, and, ironically, these widely-scattered assaults on Italian patrols, ambushes of small units, and destruction of bunkers or flak emplacements convinced even the Germans that as many as 40,000 American paratroopers were running amok in Sicily's interior. In his book about the invasion, Samuel Mitcham explained, "Spontaneously, small raiding parties led by junior officers [...] stalked through the dark countryside, creating fear and confusion among German and Italian soldiers [...] In a manner reminiscent of Indian warfare tactics of America's Old West, these stealthy raiders, many wearing war paint and with their heads shaved, lay in wait in the darkness along roads." (Mitcham, 2007, 73).

Gavin

An even greater fiasco developed with the British "Ladbroke" glider landing. An assemblage of British-made Airspeed AS.51 Horsa wooden gliders, plus a handful of American-made metal framed Waco CG-4A gliders, numbering 144 in all, left Tunisia late on July 9th, towed by 109 American C-47 Skytrain transports and 35 British A.W.41 Albemarle glider tugs. The Anglo-American leadership ordered these 1,700 men to take the Ponte Grande Bridge across the Anapo River. The commanders hoped to duplicate the crisp and well-oiled use of gliders by the Germans during the seizure of Fort Eben-Emael at the start of hostilities. Instead, they sacrificed many men for negligible gain.

Almost totally inexperienced at towing gliders, battered by gale-force winds, confused by the darkness, and alarmed by numerous bursts of flak that seemed closer in the night, the pilots released the Horsa and Waco craft too soon and too low. The airmen released most of the gliders at heights of 2,000 to 4,000 feet, often too low to gain needed lift and maneuvering room, and frequently did so before actually reaching the Sicilian coast. Approximately half of the gliders crashed into the ocean, some plunging totally beneath the waves and carrying hundreds of men to their doom. Others shattered on the surface, or managed a belly landing and floated for some time, permitting the men inside to hack their way free and find suitable wreckage to cling to. One lucky crew landed safely – though accidentally – in Malta, and another in the south Tunisian desert.

While many men drowned and Italian machine gunners on the shore killed others mercilessly as they floated helpless in the water, some managed to hold out until rescued when daylight came, showing perhaps a touch of British understatement as they did so: "'We went under almost instantly,' Flight Officer Ruby H. Dees recalled. 'When I reached the surface, the rest of the fellows were hanging on the wreckage.' An officer clinging to another fractured wing murmured to a British major, 'All is not well, Bill.'" (Atkinson, 2007, 90).

Meanwhile, the Italians shot down many of the gliders that actually reached land, scattered over a 30 mile front rather than concentrated in one place. Explosives and grenades aboard the gliders cooked off as they crashed, shattering the craft and the men inside them. Around 12 landed near the Ponte Grande, with one crashing so spectacularly that only a single man out of 30 emerged alive.

Out of 2,057 glider troops launched at the beginning of the attack, 87 men actually reached the bridge. This small force gallantly took and held the Ponte Grande for several hours, but by 4:00 p.m., the Italians wounded or killed all but 15 of the British. The British soldiers finally surrendered, and they found themselves marched off by a diminutive, swaggering Italian officer. Just a few minutes later, however, a patrol of soldiers from a Northamptonshire unit rescued them and took the Italian officer prisoner, and a band of Royal Scots Fusiliers arrived at the bridge via an overland march and took it intact, proving "Ladbroke" an utterly futile waste of human lives.

The British 8th Army under Montgomery landed on Sicily's southeast coast. In most sectors, the few coastal batteries present succumbed quickly to bombardment by destroyers and other supporting ships offshore. Elements of at least two Italian Coastal Divisions occupied the areas attacked, but did little other than skirmish lightly with the British before retreating, though they did capture some 174 British Ladbroke glider troops, along with a handful of stray American paratroopers.

A picture of Allied forces off shore

In conjunction with that, Miles Dempsey's 13th Corps landed further north on Sicily's east coast, with the 5th Division landing along the beaches designated "Acid North" just south of the city of Syracuse. Dempsey tasked them with seizing the important objective of the Syracuse-Augusta naval base, a major Italian facility and fortress in eastern Sicily. The 50th Northumbrian Division came ashore to the south at "Acid South," landing points near the city of Noto.

The rest of the British 8th Army, Oliver Leese's 30th Corps, landed along a 25 mile stretch of Sicilian coast divided into three zones, Bark East, Bark South, and Bark West, including the Pachino Peninsula at the island's southeast corner and some of the shore west of it. The 1st and 2nd Canadian Infantry Divisions landed in the Bark West sector and moved to secure Pachino Airfield. The English and Canadians faced heavy surf and difficult landing conditions in the darkness, but almost no hostile fire. By 6:45 a.m., the 8th Army found itself well-established on shore at the start of a clear, hot, sunny day.

A picture of British soldiers coming ashore

Further to the west, the U.S. 7th Army came ashore at their own designated landings, Cent – near Scoglitti, about 15 miles west of the Canadian disembarkation points – Dime – near Geta – and Joss – on a 10 mile stretch of coast flanking the town of Licata, a picturesque bluffside town. American objectives included several small airstrips within a short distance of the coast.

The U.S. 45th Infantry Division landed along the coast in the "Cent" sector, around Scoglitti. The "Thunderbirds" met little resistance from human adversaries, but suffered considerable losses during their landing from natural forces. Coming ashore through a violent, chaotic nine-foot surf, landing craft collided or smashed to pieces on jagged, half-submerged rocks, drowning scores of men. The Americans pushed inland, taking ground rapidly as the Italians fled in wild disorder or surrendered, as at San Croce Camerina: "When [Lieutenant Colonel Felix L.] Sparks arrived in the village, he was greeted by dozens of white flags fluttering from windows. Five hundred Italian soldiers had given up without the loss of a single American life. 'Those goddamn Italians came right out with their hands up,' Sparks recalled, 'with their bags packed, ready to go to the States.'" (Kershaw, 2012, 36).

The 3rd Infantry Division landed in the Joss sector, seizing Licata and pushing inland. The U.S. 1st Infantry Division – the famous and relatively experienced "Big Red One," named for its unit insignia of a crimson number one on an olive green shield, came ashore in the center of the American landings near Gela. The battle of Gela on July 10th, continuing into the 11th as the Germans launched a counterattack against the beachhead, represented the only serious fighting during the initial invasion.

The 1st and 4th Ranger Battalions, among the first American soldiers ashore, encountered minefields in addition to machine gun fire from the Italian defenders and artillery fire from heights commanding the beach and town from a distance of several miles. One luckless Ranger officer, in the lead, stepped on a mine which blew his torso open. He turned to the men behind him, his beating heart exposed, and exclaimed, "I've had it." Other Rangers suffered wounds from exploding mines, and the Italians successfully set off demolition charges that destroyed the Gela pier. After a surprisingly vigorous firefight, the Rangers ejected the Italians – men of the 18th Coastal Brigade under Major Rubellino – from Gela, taking 200 prisoners in the process. The 26th Infantry Regiment leapfrogged inland to take the tactically useful high ground near Ponte Olivo, while the 16th Infantry Regiment took another commanding position at Piano Lupo, though only after a fierce struggle against determined Italian soldiers in a string of machine-gun nests.

In the meantime, the Italian artillery swept the beach with shells so persistently that the "Big Red One" abandoned the idea of offloading their artillery there. Instead, the landing craft carrying the vital guns shifted to the Joss landing zone to the west, greatly delaying their deployment.

By mid-morning, the Italians launched a major three-pronged counterattack, including troops from the Livorno Division. Dozens of Renault R-35 and Fiat 3000 light tanks supported each of the infantry columns as they advanced courageously against the dug-in Americans. No U.S. tanks yet supported the infantry due to difficulties in clearing the minefields while under Italian artillery fire. Light scouting aircraft deployed from the ships offshore served as spotters, despite being hunted ruthlessly by prowling Messerschmitt Bf-109D fighters. With their aid, the USS *Shubrick*, USS *Savannah*, USS *Boise*, and HMS *Abercrombie* fired their guns at a range of ten miles and successfully destroyed a number of Italian tanks. The Rangers then worked their way forward aggressively with bazookas, using the broken ground to get close to the Italian tanks and destroy more of them. With their routes of advance clogged by shattered, burning hulks, and with fierce fire directed at them by the Americans, the Italian soldiers finally withdrew, though not before taking a handful of prisoners from the 26th Infantry Regiment.

Scarcely had the Italians retreated when the ominous, faceted shapes of Panzer IV tanks appeared amid clouds of dust, advancing from the north at about 1 PM. The Hermann Goering Division's panzers attacked the 16th Infantry Division at Piano Lupo and overran their positions, then continued down towards the beachhead itself. At this point, heavy fire from the warships offshore brought the German tanks to a temporary halt.

Truck-mounted infantry of the 15th Panzergrenadier Division, supported by the full force of 17 Panzer VI Tiger tanks, also launched an attack, capturing the entire 1st Battalion of the U.S. 180th Infantry Regiment. They were finally halted when the Tigers entangled themselves in an olive grove. The day ended indecisively as the Germans pulled back slightly to regroup and Patton's 2nd Armored Division put their first M4 Shermans ashore despite moderately effective bombing attacks by the Luftwaffe.

A Sherman tank on Sicily after the landing

A picture of materials being towed ashore

The Battle of Gela continued on the next day, July 11th, 1943. A pleasantly mild morning soon turned into a scene of chaos and mayhem as over 30 Panzer IVs and 30 Panzer IIIs rolled forward against the 26th Infantry Regiment, smashing through it amid a storm of bullets and shells and rolling down towards the beach. Out of 60 M4 Shermans then ashore, only four remained serviceable, the remainder having thrown their tracks. Patton himself landed as the German tanks advanced closer and closer to Gela and the beachhead, swaggering about fearlessly and barking orders.

The tide turned gradually as Patton called for the ships offshore to shell the German tanks. Directed with deadly accuracy by spotters on the ground and in the air, the naval gunners destroyed tank after tank. Daring American soldiers, many of them Rangers, worked close to the steel giants to fire bazooka rounds into their underside or engine compartments. When the Germans finally began to withdraw at 2:00 p.m., they left 43 tanks behind, a figure that both U.S. Army and Wehrmacht records independently corroborate. Among these, 10 of the mighty Tigers had suffered destruction from naval shells. Bazooka teams accounted for six Panzer III and IV tanks out of the total. Patton described the failed attack as "the shortest Blitzkrieg in history" (Macintyre, 2010, 245), and German losses numbered 630 men killed or wounded while the Americans sustained 175 killed and 665 wounded.

Ultimately, many far-reaching consequences followed from Operation Husky. The Italians ousted Mussolini, leading to his imprisonment, rescue by the Nazis, and reestablishment of a rump Fascist state in northern Italy. For their part, the Germans used the time taken by the Allies in expelling them from Sicily to occupy much of Italy in detail, creating a new front.

Of course, the Allies also gained some advantages. They carried out the amphibious assault with superb professionalism, even if the accompanying airborne drops proved catastrophically bungled. Perhaps most importantly, the Allied forces gained invaluable experience in amphibious operations that would later be put to good use during the D-Day landings in Normandy a year later. The U.S. Army also gained the battle experience needed to quickly become one of the most formidable Allied armies during the war.

The Mediterranean route also opened for Lend-Lease shipments to the Soviet Union, increasing the flood of materiel by 27% annually. On top of that, the USSR also benefited immensely by the removal of many German divisions earmarked for a fresh 1943 offensive – 17 redeployed to the Balkans and Greece alone – which also gutted Hitler's Kursk offensive. With so many men and vehicles stripped from the Eastern Front, the balance tipped from deep uncertainty to a steady (though brutally costly) Soviet advance.

In fact, Operation Husky interrupted Operation Citadel in southern Russia at its most crucial moment. The Germans had penetrated two of three Soviet defensive lines and were poised to encircle and capture another vast horde of Russians. Had Citadel carried forward, the Wehrmacht stood a good chance of regaining the initiative in the east, pushing the Soviets back in a series of fresh defeats. Instead, Hitler decided to defend Italy, allowing the Soviets to counterattack and gain the initiative for themselves, grabbing momentum that they never relinquished.

Operation Overlord

D-Day is the one event of World War II that all nations attach utmost significance to. Today it is remembered for spelling the beginning of the end for Nazi Germany, but it was the most complex war-time operation ever executed, and Eisenhower himself was aware there was a high probability that the invasion would be defeated, which would set the Allies back at least a year in Western Europe if not longer.

To put the difficulties the Allies faced into context, the Normandy invasion was the first successful opposed landings across the English Channel in over eight centuries. Strategically, the campaign led to the loss of the German position in most of France and the secure establishment of a new major front. In a wider context, the Normandy landings helped the Soviets on the Eastern front, who were facing the bulk of the German forces and, to a certain extent, contributed to the shortening of the conflict there.

During the first half of 1944, the Americans and British began a massive buildup of men and resources in England, while the military leaders devised an enormous and complex amphibious invasion of Western Europe. Though the Allies theoretically had several different staging grounds for an attack on different sides of the continent, the most obvious place for an invasion was just across the English Channel from Britain into France. And though the Allies used misinformation to deceive the Germans, Hitler's men built an extensive network of coastal fortifications throughout France to protect against just such an invasion. Largely under the supervision of Rommel, the Germans constructed the "Atlantic Wall", across which reinforced concrete pillboxes for German defenders were built close to the beaches for infantry to use machine guns and anti-tank artillery. Large obstacles were placed along the beaches to effectively block tanks on the ground, while mines and underwater obstacles were planted to stop landing craft from getting close enough.

The Atlantic Wall necessitated an elaborate and complex invasion plan that would ensure the men who landed wouldn't be fish in a barrel. Thus, the Allies began drawing up an elaborate battle plan that would include naval and air bombardment, paratroopers, and even inflatable tanks that would be able to fire on fortifications from the coastline, all while landing over 150,000 men across 50 miles of French beaches. And that was just the beginning; the Allies intended to create a beachhead that could support an artificially constructed dock, after which nearly 1 million men would be ferried to France for the final push of the war.

A sense of fear and foreboding marred the weeks and months in the build up to the invasion. Churchill was aghast at Eisenhower's bombing plan to accompany the landings, which would have resulted in the deaths of between 80,000 and 150,000 French civilians. It would have been an outrageous number of civilian casualties, and more French citizens killed by Allied bombing than had lost their lives in four years of German occupation. Churchill felt it was better to continue the bombing of Germany rather than inflict terrible casualties upon their French allies in support of what may be a doomed invasion. Just months before the planned invasion of France, Allied forces had landed at Anzio, just south of Rome. Almost immediately, the Allied landing force was halted and almost driven back into the sea. Churchill himself had been a leading player in the invasion of Gallipoli in 1915, a debacle which almost cost him his career. The idea of landing on the heavily defended Normandy coast filled Churchill with fear. On one occasion, just weeks before the launch of *Overlord,* the Prime Minister was heard to say, ""Why are we doing this? Why do we not land instead in a friendly territory, the territory of our oldest ally? Why do we not land in Portugal?"

Churchill was not alone. Many of the British military planners had felt a cross channel invasion "smacked of a seaborne Somme". Churchill had, however, persuaded the U.S. to give priority to the war in Europe, a position which caused many difficulties for Roosevelt. Pearl Harbor had outraged America and inflamed popular opinion against Japan, yet American attitudes towards Germany and Italy were far more ambivalent, due to the large proportion of American citizens with German or Italian heritage. However, at the somewhat bizarre Rattle Conference, described as a combination of intensive study and a 1920s themed house party, organized by Lord Louis Mountbatten, the assembled company settled upon Normandy as the invasion destination. Although further from Germany, it offered the Allies the chance to capture two major ports, Cherbourg and Le Harve.

Facing these obstacles, it is perhaps best to consider what the alliance of millions of soldiers and support personnel were able to accomplish. On June 5, 1944, an armada of some 7,000 ships crossed the Channel towards the Normandy peninsula. Above it, 1,400 troop transports and 11,590 military aircraft of various types (along with 3,700 fighters) supported the landings. The following day, 175,000 soldiers were landed. The men who successfully invaded on D-Day earn all the credit they've since been given, but it was made possible by the enormous effort displayed in the planning and organization of the invasion.

At the outbreak of World War II, none of the belligerents could have expected to make an opposed amphibious invasion on the large scale of *Operation Neptune*, the codename for the Normandy landings on D-Day. Yet, with the early stages of the war going badly for both sides, amphibious landings became a crucial strategy. The prospect of a large scale invasion came only after the Allies were forcibly ejected from the European continent. Dr. Andrew Gordon, in his article *'The greatest military armada ever launched'*, reminded readers of the analogy Napoleon used to characterize the European powers as elephants, while describing Britain as a whale. The metaphor stood true in 1940, as Britain was able to slink back into the sea and live to fight another day, while the German war machine was left standing on the shores of France.

Germany dominated the land, while Britain was safe across the Channel so long as it could dominate the air above Britain and the seas around it. Eventually, either of the powers would have to learn how to enter and dominate the other power's theater of influence. Upon American entry into the war, U.S. planners pushed for a landing in Europe and determined push towards Germany, ideally in 1943. The British viewed such a proposal as premature, but they established a planning staff in July 1943 under the command of Admiral Bertram Ramsay, to lay the groundwork for invasion.

Ramsay

Under Ramsay, the areas of the Normandy coast between the rivers Vire and Orne were chosen as the landing zone, and it was under Ramsay that the ideas behind the MULBERRY harbors and the ingenious pipeline-under-the-ocean (PLUTO) were conceived. Churchill claims to have thought of MULBERRY harbors first, however, the most likely inventor is Commodore John Hughes-Hallet, known to have stated: "if we can't capture a port, we must take one with us." The problem was as huge in scale as it was simple in principle: the Allies needed to prefabricate a harbor the size of Dover in England, then tow it across the Channel and install it at the invasion beaches. What was needed was a sheltered, deep-water anchorage within which large ships could speedily unload supplies and reinforcements.

The solution was the MULBERRY harbors. Ground-breaking and complex, the harbors were comprised of 146 concrete caissons, to be sunk along an outer perimeter to act as breakwaters and ensure calm seas within the harbors. Prior to the creation of the MULBERRY harbors, any invasion which failed to secure a major port almost immediately would be doomed to failure, thus the reason the Germans had chosen ports as the location of their heaviest defenses. For a defending army the options were simple, hold all major ports until the unsupported invaders are repelled, exhausted, destroyed or run out of ammo, or destroy all major ports beyond short term repair. The MULBERRYS made German holding or destruction of French ports more of a nuisance than a disaster.

Ambulances coming ashore from the Mulberry harbors

Upon his appointment as Supreme Allied Commander in January 1944, Eisenhower wasted little time in demanding the scale of the landings be increased from three divisions to five. This step had far reaching ramifications in terms of resources and transport. Extra landing craft, support vessels, mine sweepers and bombardment vessels would be needed in a hurry to match the expansion of the invasion plans. Luckily, the U.S. forces were able to muster the extra ships needed.

In the early spring of 1944, the final stages of *Neptune* took shape. Landings would occur at five separate beaches in divisional strength. Prior to this, Beach Reconnaissance Parties were covertly landed at the five sites on dark nights to ascertain the nature, defenses and gradients of the beaches. The day before the invasion, D-Day -1, Allied minesweepers would have to be visible to the German defenses in order to complete their duties successfully. Either due to bad weather, German withdrawals or poor patrolling, the minesweepers were not detected. It was at Ramsay's headquarters that Eisenhower and the other senior commanders spent the final days and hours before the decision to go was given.

In the early hours of the morning of June 4, the decision was made upon the advice of meteorologists. In the days before the decision to launch, the weather approaching the Normandy beaches had been the worst for years, so bad that a landing would be all but impossible. Landings could be undertaken for just 10 days per month due to the tides and the need for a full moon to aid navigation. Delaying the landings in the early part of June would have meant that another attempt could not have been made for at least two weeks, and with well over 150,000 troops already on their ships waiting to go, that situation was not acceptable. Luckily for the Allies, chief meteorologist, Captain Stagg, with the aid of a meteorological station on the west coast of Ireland, was able to inform the assembled commanders that a brief clearing in the weather for a number of hours looked likely.

Ramsay, head of Naval affairs, informed Eisenhower that the Royal Navy would do whatever was asked of it, Montgomery, commander of the ground forces favored immediate action, while Leigh-Mallory, commander of the air-fleet was hesitant, worried that the bad weather would limit the support his air force could give to the landing troops. After a brief pause of no more than a few seconds, Eisenhower simply said "Let's go". With that, the largest invasion fleet ever assembled began its journey towards the Normandy coast.

From the very beginning of June 6, 1944, events did not go as the Allies had planned. In the first operations of the day, a cloud of Allied aircraft flew overhead, targeting German troop concentrations, infrastructure and fortifications throughout the Normandy countryside. On D-Day alone, Allied air forces flew over 14,000 sorties, compared to just 100 for the Luftwaffe, a clear sign of the total superiority the Allies enjoyed.

The Allied airborne assault in the early morning hours of June 6, 1944 proved to be as full of complexity, drama, heroism, confusion, loss and effort as the beach landings that followed. However, despite the heroism, the airborne assaults did not go to plan. The final plan for the Allied airborne invasion called on the 82nd Airborne to drop its regiments on either side of the Merderet River. The paratroopers would control the plateau west of the river and two major roads north of the Douve River before it joined the Merderet. East of the river, the division's theater of operations included the town of Ste-Mere-Eglise, five roads, a rail road and two small towns. The 101st Airborne's theatre covered about 400 square miles east of Ste-Mere-Eglise-Carentan Road. The 101st was charged with opening the route for the 4th Division of Utah to come off the beach. The fortunes of the 101st and 4th divisions were complementary. The 4th relied on the paratroopers to clear as much German artillery as possibly to allow the successful invasion of Utah, while the 101st needed the 4th's armor to come ashore to add weight to its attacking prowess.

On the British side, the 5th Parachute Brigade prevented German use of Pegasus Bridge, while the 3rd Parachute Brigade were charged with seizing four other bridges. The 6th Airlanding

Brigade came in by glider to provide light vehicles, heavy machine guns and artillery. In one of the most famous and spectacular missions of the whole campaign, D Company, 2nd Battalion, the Oxfordshire and Buckinghamshire Light infantry, took Pegasus bridge after the most magnificent piece of piloting of the war, in which their glider pilots managed to guide them within yards of their target bridge. The attackers poured out of their battered gliders, completely surprising the German defenders, and took the bridges within 10 minutes. It was in this action where the first Allied casualty of D-Day was suffered and also where the first house to be liberated in France was situated.

At the top left of the image is Pegasus Bridge. It's clear how remarkably close the glider pilots managed to land.

Cafe Gondree at Pegasus Bridge claims to be the first house to be liberated in France.

However, while the weather was good enough to carry out the attacks on June 6, the early morning hours had low cloud-cover, making it hard for the Allied aircraft to locate and hit their targets. The Allies' planes mostly missed German fortifications on their bombing runs, and tens of thousands of paratroopers who were to land directly behind German lines were dropped out of place due to poor visibility. The only true advantage the paratrooper drops had for the Allies was that the scattered nature of the paratroopers confused the German defenders.

The contribution of Allied air power to the success of the invasion did not end with the actions of D-Day. Allied air power smashed the remaining Luftwaffe in France as it moved forward to meet the landings, and it also targeted roads, infrastructure and German supply lines. Coupled with Allied deciphering of German codes, the air forces were able to inflict terrible damage. On June 9, the Allies deciphered German communications that revealed the exact location of Panzer Group West. The following day, the Allies destroyed the panzer group's communications entirely, killing 17 staff officers, including the Chief of Staff. Without this supremacy in the skies, the landings might have faced stiff opposition from the Luftwaffe, which would have been devastating.

The span of the landings covered an area of 55 miles, a length large enough for the Allies to ensure a funnel of resupply could be held. As previously mentioned, amphibious landings are one of the most difficult aspects of warfare, no more so than during the Second World War, where technological advances, such as the machine gun, mortars and other portable weapons capable of inflicting terrible losses, allowed a relatively small number of defenders to inflict horrific casualties upon a landing force.

Due to the reinforced German positions and heavy artillery pieces with which the Allies faced, the British laid on a two hour bombardment before attempting a landing. Unfortunately for the U.S. forces, particularly on Omaha, Bradley felt a 20 minute bombardment would be sufficient, relying on the Army Air Force to launch a massive attack. But such an attack had been made impossible for the Air Force due to the low cloud cover that had resulted in bombers entirely missing the German positions below. Bradley further compounded the impending misery and torment for his ground troops by completely disregarding the advice of Major-General Pete Corlett, a veteran of successful Pacific amphibious landings. Bradley's attitude was far from open minded and dismissed Corlett's advice by saying "anything that happened in the Pacific was strictly bush-league stuff." Bradley's decision not to employ adequate naval bombardment robbed his troops of crucial support. For example, a Brooklyn type cruiser, as was available to

Bradley on D-Day, could fire 1,500 five inch shells in ten minutes, and when directed by spotter aircraft, its fire was deadly accurate. Yet Bradley, with his deep suspicion and prejudices against the U.S. Navy, remained ignorant. Nevertheless, and to the relief of the U.s. troops at Omaha, when it became obvious the landings there were teetering on failure, a number of destroyer skippers moved their vessels so close to the shore that they risked beaching to support the hard-pressed troops.

Landing at Utah Beach

In the narrative of D-Day, Omaha Beach has become the best known part of the attacks among Americans, due to the various difficulties the Americans faced there before managing to succeed. But it's essential to remember that each of the 5 beaches were their own story, and largely forgotten is the remarkable success of the American landings at Utah Beach, which were easier in comparison to the other four landing zones.

The 82nd and 101st Airborne, dropped the night before the landings, had ensured little German resistance remained. In one of the finest and most famous pieces of soldiering of the day, 101st

Airborne Lieutenant Richard Winters, of Band of Brothers fame, almost single-handedly took out a German battery. On the beaches, despite an abnormally strong tidal current which swept forces 2,000 yards further south than planned, the landings at Utah encountered little opposition. From the outset, everything went right for the Americans. 28 out of the 32 amphibious tanks made it ashore, with the only major obstacle facing them being the sand dunes and flooded fields of Normandy. Even by noon, the 4th Infantry was able to advance from the beaches and expand their theater of command into the Normandy countryside. The 4th's casualty rate illustrates the success of Utah: 197 casualties out of a total landing force of 23,000 men.

Aerial view of Omaha Beach on D-Day

If the landings at Utah could be described as easy, those at Omaha were chronically bad. Due to the aforementioned failure to reinforce Omaha Beach, despite Rommel's insistence, the U.S. Army encountered just two battalions, rather than the ten which should have been in position. Those two divisions, however, were more than enough to guarantee the U.S. Army one of its worst days in history.

Despite the fact the Germans had just two battalions in position, the landings at Omaha were a disaster. Some military operations are dogged by bad luck, and Omaha is certainly one of those. To begin with, the initial air bombardment completely missed its intended target, and the naval bombardment of just 20 minutes hardly damaged any German defenses. General Bradley had told his men, "You men should consider yourself lucky. You are going to have ringside seats for the greatest show on earth." However, Rear Admiral John L. Hall, in reference to the lack of naval bombardment, countered, "It's a crime to send me on the biggest amphibious attack in history with such inadequate naval gunfire support.

Bradley

Things went wrong even before troops hit Omaha Beach, but inadequacies in naval and air bombardment weren't the only problems. The invasion called for deploying inflatable tanks on the water that could provide cover for the infantry, but the officer in charge of releasing the amphibious tanks panicked and sent them into the deep swells of the Channel, causing 29 of the 34 tanks immediately sinking to the bottom. Finally, since the landing came at low tide, the troops were forced to move across 300 yards of water, followed by 100 yards of beach, steep dunes, and finally swamp, minefield and barbed wire. If a soldier had managed to run the gauntlet and survive, he then faced a climb up the cliffs to the high ground.

The result was, unsurprisingly, a slaughter. Much of the first wave of troops was gunned down before they could get out of the water. Machine gun and rifle fire pinned down those landing craft not destroyed by underwater mines, while those pinned down in the dunes, many gravely injured, were in no position to return any meaningful fire. After these first landing vehicles kept landing along a narrow strip unsheltered against the German defenders, similar landings were suspended during the morning hours of the operation.

Only the ingenuity of the on-looking destroyer captains, who risked beaching their craft to aid the unfortunate troops, provided some relief. Before sun had set on June 6, over 2,500 U.S. troops were dead, with some units incurring up to 95% casualties. Only thanks to the efforts of low ranking officers and NCOs did the U.S. avoid complete annihilation on Omaha. Pressing through the unimaginable fire, a few managed to begin clearing German defenses.

Omaha Beach on the afternoon of D-Day

Recovering the dead at Omaha

By the end of D-Day, troops on Omaha had only managed to grab two small beachheads, isolated from each other no less, making it the least successful landing spot among the five beaches. It would take a few more days for the Allies to firmly consolidate its hold on Omaha Beach and begin to push inland, after which a MULBERRY harbor was placed there. Somewhat fittingly, the harbor experienced the worst storms in the area in decades, and three days of storms irreparably wrecked the harbor on June 22.

Nevertheless, the preciously bought beach became the main supply zone for the invasion of France. Over the next three months, the Allies used Omaha Beach to land a million tons of supplies, 100,000 vehicles, and 600,000 men, while evacuating nearly 100,000 casualties.

Using Omaha Beach after D-Day

Landing on Gold Beach

The aims of the British landings at Gold were to establish a link between the British and the U.S. forces at Omaha. Due in part to the heavy naval bombardment of Gold Beach, the British forces were able to overrun the German defenses in most places, although they suffered heavy losses in attacks on German strong points such as Le Hamel. For the British it was a success, but certainly not a smooth, unopposed ride as the following quote shows: "We hit two mines going in…They didn't stop us, although the ramp was damaged and an officer standing on it was killed. The first man off was a commando sergeant in full kit. He disappeared like a stone into six feet of water. The beach was strewn with wreckage, a blazing tank, bundles of blankets and kit, bodies and bits of bodies. One bloke near me was blown in half and his lower half collapsed in a bloody heap on the sand."

Like other sectors, Gold Beach did not go entirely according to plan, mostly because the tidal waters that day left the water levels higher than planned. Engineers who were meant to remove some of the obstacles found that British ships were passing over them, which was helpful in some ways and harmful in others. As a contingency, the amphibious tanks had to be landed on the beach, providing necessary cover for the infantry.

After about 3 hours, the British had successfully established a beachhead on Gold Beach. The British division was able to advance through the suburbs of the town of Bayeux after penetrating the German defenses, one of the few Norman cities to fall without a fight. Of the 25,000 men who landed on Gold Beach, only about 400 became casualties. "Hobart's Funnies", which had been the subject of ridicule, proved invaluable at Gold Beach, with the different modified tanks clearing minefields, bridging ditches, and creating trackways across the sands to facilitate movement on and off the beaches.

By the end of D-Day, the British soldiers who landed on Gold Beach were about 6 miles inland, allowing them to link up with the Canadians on Juno Beach. Moreover, the success at Gold was crucial to the embattled U.S. Army on Omaha, because it drew German fighters away from the struggling Americans.

Landing on Juno Beach

The 3rd Canadian Division landing at Juno Beach experienced much of the same success as the British, albeit with higher casualties. Due to the Canadians arriving late on the beach, the tide was high, ensuring Rommel's underwater mines were able to inflict as much damage as possible. No fewer than 20 of the 24 lead landing craft were damaged or destroyed. The German army also managed to put up stern defenses around Juno.

Like the British however, the Canadians had the foresight to land their amphibious tanks on the beach when circumstances required it. With the help of these tanks providing cover, the Canadians were able to flank the German defenders, breaching the strong outer layer of German defenses relatively quickly in the northern section of the beach.

The Canadian soldiers landing in the south had it worse. As the 8th Brigade's reserve battalion, Le Régiment de la Chaudière, headed to shore, mines badly damaged their landing crafts, and the soldiers lost almost all of their supplies swimming to shore. With Canadian units pinned down in the south, reserves that landed less than an hour after the initial attacks found to their horror that the German strongholds defending their sector had not been reduced. The 400 man No. 48 (Royal Marine) Commando lost nearly 200 men within seconds of landing.

Despite suffering a total of about 1,000 casualties, the Canadians were able to pour through and push inland. German forces were unable to mount a counterattack until the brutal, murderous Waffen SS Hitlerjugend arrived the following day. By then, the Canadians were well positioned enough to absorb and survive the vicious counterattack. While they received heavy casualties, killed, wounded and captured, with many of the captured brutally murdered by the SS, the Canadians held their ground and pressed on towards the main provincial town of Caen.

Coming ashore on Sword Beach

The Sword landings were, in comparison to those at Juno, quite easy. Generally, the heavy naval bombardment quelled German resistance, except the heavily defended stronghold of La Breche, which held on for up to three hours. The men on Sword Beach were the only ones to face a determined German counterattack, which came from the 21st Panzer division. But air superiority and effective defenses ensured that the German counterattack almost entirely fizzled out, and the Germans that made progress were eventually compelled to retreat by the end of the day anyway.

Still, two main problems confronted the British attackers. As British forces piled onto the beach, those at the front struggled to break through some German lines, creating a backlog on the beach that left some of the British wide open to indiscriminate German artillery, which inflicted significant loss of life and panic. The 3rd British Division, after landing on Sword, was tasked with meeting up with the British Airborne, which had taken the strategically important Pegasus Bridge in one of the few airborne operations that was successful on D-Day. From there, the

British units were to move south towards Caen, eventually linking up with the British and Canadians landing on Gold and Juno Beaches.

However, with British forces massing outside Caen, the plan began to go wrong. Due to the congestion on Sword Beach, the supporting armor was unable to reach the infantry further south. Further compounding the British problem, the heavily defended Hillman fortress stood directly in their path. A particularly bloody and drawn out battle ensued which lasted for most of the afternoon. As British troops pushed towards Caen they encountered elements of the 21st Panzer Division, ensuring Caen would not fall until the middle of July. Considering the varying degrees of success on all the landing beaches, it is perhaps a blessing in disguise that the taking of Caen was delayed, as it allowed Allied forces to better coordinate their attack against the well defended city.

By the end of D-Day, the Allies had managed to successfully land 170,000 men: over 75,000 on the British and Canadian beaches, 57,000 on the American beaches, and over 24,000 airborne troops. Thanks to Allied deception, the German army had failed to react to prevent the Allies from making the most of their landings. Just one division, the Hitlerjugend, would arrive the following day. Despite a fearsome and bloody day, the majority of the Allied forces had held their nerve, and most importantly, achieved their objectives. This ensured *Operation Overlord* was ultimately successful, and victory in Europe would be achieved within less than a year.

Operation Overlord aimed to have the Allies reach the Seine River within 3 months of D-Day, and it's a testament to the men who fought and served on D-Day that the goal was reached early. To do so, the Allies overcame firm resistance from the Germans, atrocious weather that limited resupply for the Allies, and the difficult terrain of Normandy, which included endless hedgerows providing hidden cover. And the Allies reached their objective ahead of time despite the fact the objectives of D-Day were not entirely met; the Allies had not captured Caen, St-lo or Bayeux on the first day.

Nevertheless, the landings were clearly a resounding success. Casualties were significantly smaller than those expected by commanders, and the significance of D-Day to the morale of the Western world, much of it under German domination, cannot be underestimated. For France, Poland, Czechoslovakia, Belgium, Holland and more, who had suffered over four years of occupation, the great democracies were finally coming to their rescue. American, British, Canadian, Polish, Commonwealth, Greek, Belgian, Dutch and Norwegian soldiers, sailors, and airmen all participated in the Battle for Normandy, which saw the Allies on the banks of the Seine River just 80 days after D-Day.

Churchill was not overstating the achievements of *Operation Overlord* when he described the plan "the greatest thing we have ever attempted". The greatest armada the world had ever seen had landed 170,000 soldiers on the heavily defended beaches of Normandy in just 24 hours. More remarkable was the fact that the operation was a success on every major level. Deception, tactical surprise and overwhelming force had contributed to the establishment of an adequate beachhead. Confusion and dissent had stopped the Germans massing for any great counterattack. The Atlantic Wall which Hitler had placed so much faith in had been breached, and the race to Paris was on.

Online Resources

Other World War II titles by Charles River Editors

Other titles about World War II on Amazon

Bibliography

Adcock, Al. *WWII US Landing Craft in Action.* Carrollton, 2003.

Atwater, Charles B. *Soviet Amphibious Operations in the Black Sea, 1941-1943.* Web, 1995. **https://www.globalsecurity.org/military/library/report/1995/ACB.htm**

Dyer, Vice Admiral George C. *The Amphibians Came to Conquer.* Washington, D.C., 1972.

Gebhardt, James F. *Leavenworth Papers Number 17: The Petsamo-Kirkenes Operation: Soviet Breakthrough and Pursuit in the Arctic, October 1944.* Forth Leavenworth, 1989.

Gladkov, Vasily Fedorovich. *Десант на Эльтиген.* [Assault Landing at Eltigen.] Moscow, 1972. [Quote translated from Russian by author.]

Griffith, Brigadier General Samuel B. *The Battle for Guadalcanal.* New York, 1980.

Krulak, Victor H. *First to Fight: An Inside View of the Marine Corps.* Annapolis, 1984.

Mercey, Arch A. *Sea, Surf, and Hell: The U.S. Coast Guard in World War II.* New York, 1945.

Melzer, Walther. *Kampf um die Baltischen Inseln, 1917 – 1941 – 1944.* Neckargemund, 1960. [Quotes translated from German by author.]

Merriam, Ray (ed.). *Japanese Landing Craft of World War II: U.S. Naval Technical Mission to Japan.* Bennington, 2006.

Military Publishing House. *Military Encyclopedic Dictionary.* Moscow, 1983.

Newell, Reg. *Operation Goodtime and the Battle of the Treasury Islands, 1943.* Jefferson, 2012.

Vandegrift, Archer A. *Once a Marine: The Memoirs of General A.A. Vandegrift, United States Marine Corps.* New York, 1964.

Walling, Michael G. *Bloodstained Sands: U.S. Amphibious Operations in World War II.* New York, 2017.

Free Books by Charles River Editors

We have brand new titles available for free most days of the week. To see which of our titles are currently free, click on this link.

Discounted Books by Charles River Editors

We have titles at a discount price of just 99 cents everyday. To see which of our titles are currently 99 cents, click on this link.

Made in the USA
Las Vegas, NV
29 August 2023

76793398R00056